MAINLINE TO THE FUTURE

MAINLINE TO THE FUTURE

Congregations for the
21st Century

Jackson W. Carroll

Westminster John Knox Press
Louisville, Kentucky

Scripture quotations, unless otherwise indicated, are from the New Revised Standard Version of the Bible, copyright © 1989 by the Division of Christian Education of the National Council of the Churches of Christ in the U.S.A., and used by permission.

Lyrics for "Yahweh" by Andy Park ©1994 Mercy/Vineyard Publishing. All rights reserved. Used by permission.

Book design by Sharon Adams
Cover design by Mark Abrams

First edition
Published by Westminster John Knox Press
Louisville, Kentucky

This book is printed on acid-free paper that meets the American National Standards Institute Z39.48 standard.∞

PRINTED IN THE UNITED STATES OF AMERICA

00 01 02 03 04 05 06 07 08 09 — 10 9 8 7 6 5 4 3 2 1

A catalog card for this book may be obtained from the Library of Congress

ISBN 0-664-22253-6

For

Caroline Anne Strumph
Matthew Sumner Strumph
Philip Jackson Whitcomb
Anne Carroll Whitcomb
Genevieve Auriol Whitcomb
Isabel MacNair Whitcomb

Contents

Introduction

In the late nineteen hundreds, the turn of a new century stirred thoughts of the future as it does today, with the added excitement today of a new millennium. At that time, Edward Bellamy (1888) wrote one of the most popular novels of the day. In *Looking Backward,* he gave a prognostication of what he thought the twentieth century would hold. As the book unfolds, a thirty-year-old man falls asleep in 1877 and does not awaken until the year 2000. A twentieth-century host explains the "new" American society to him. It is egalitarian, free of class conflict and the subordination of women. Productivity is high and leisure abundant. He is glad to see that "there were no lawyers," but is also concerned to know what has happened to churches. Has a revolution taken place there too? His host tells him that Americans still observe Sundays and that there are churches.

> "As to hearing a sermon today, if you wish to do so, you could either go to church or hear it here at home."
> "How am I to hear it if I stay at home?"
> "Simply by accompanying us to the music room at the proper hour and selecting an easy chair. There are some who still prefer to hear sermons in church, but most of our preaching, like our musical performances, is not in public, but delivered rather in acoustically secured chambers connected by wire with subscribers' houses. [Note that Bellamy's book preceded radio and television by many years.] If you prefer to go to a church, I shall be glad to accompany you, but I really don't believe that you are likely to hear anywhere a better discourse than you will at home. I see by the paper that Mr. Barton is to preach this morning, and he preaches only by telephone, and to audiences often reaching 150,000."[1]

What Bellamy's latter-day Rip Van Winkle discovered in his fictional account of the year 2000 bears only a partial resemblance to today's reality. Perhaps the televangelists come closest to realizing his vision. Nonetheless, the young man would have found much at which to marvel, especially in the variety of new and innovative forms of religious organizations that populate the American scene. If one is at all attentive to the present ecclesiastical scene he or she is aware that, across all denominational traditions, not just in independent congregations, new forms of congregational life and new challenges to established ecclesial practices are emerging. Consider the following signs of change:

- "Seeker" churches, "cell" churches, "mall" churches, "seven-day-a-week" churches, "next" churches—whatever we choose to call these typically large, nontraditional congregations—are probably the most visible and talked about new ecclesial form of the last twenty years. Willow Creek Community Church in Illinois is the best known of these, and it has spawned numerous imitators in both evangelical and mainline Protestant congregations. According to management consultant Peter Drucker (1990), who prefers to call these churches "pastoral churches," and who serves as a mentor to many of their leaders, they are "the only social institution [in America] that is healthy and growing."

- Worship practices, including liturgy, music, and preaching, are in great flux. Some seek to reclaim classical liturgical practices in churches that have traditionally been "low" church in liturgical style. Others, especially influenced by the "seeker church" movement, throw out traditional liturgical practices, believing them to be out of touch with the Baby Boomers and Generation Xers who have left the churches in significant numbers in recent years. Many congregations have kept traditional services intact but have introduced alternative worship as a way of satisfying different constituencies. Such experiments frequently lead to conflicts—some have called them "worship wars"—as also have efforts to alter traditional language about God, rewrite hymn texts, or drop well-loved hymns that some now find offensive because of their language or imagery.

- The explosion in recent years of small groups, often though not always part of larger congregations, is a related ecclesial development. In his study of small groups, Robert Wuthnow (1994) found that over 40 percent of Americans say they are involved in some sort of small group on a regular basis, the majority of which are religious or spiritual in character—Bible study groups, prayer and faith-sharing groups, twelve-step groups, and so forth. Such groups are part of a rediscovery of spirituality that places the emphasis on journey rather than place.

- Akin to the small-group movement but deserving mention in their own right are Basic Christian Communities, spawned by Latin American liberation theology but also finding expression in American counterparts, especially the Womanchurch movement (Winter et al. 1994), as well as in the growth of house churches and other small Christian communities in or outside congregations and parishes.

- Or again, there are those congregations that stand in the liturgical-sacramental traditions that become charismatic and adopt Pentecostal practices. In contrast, a Pentecostal congregation in Georgia leaves the Assemblies of God to become Episcopalian; and a group of evangelical Christians establishes a number of new congregations affiliated with the Antiochian Orthodox Archdiocese.

- Pentecostal practices are also having a significant impact on relatively staid middle- and working-class African-American congregations, especially in the African Methodist Episcopal churches. This neo-Pentecostal movement, as it is called, combines a deep Pentecostal piety with involvement in progressive politics and political activism, including a particularly strong concern for the plight of African-American men.

- Catholic Christians are recognizing that traditional geographic parishes are fast becoming history; that parishes of the future will consist of many smaller, intentional, and (given the growing shortage of priests) mostly lay-led groups where people gather on the basis of mutual interests and faith commitments, not by virtue of where they happen to live. The shortage of priests is not only fueling strong pleas for the ordination of women and for priestly celibacy to be made optional, but is also opening the door to new patterns of leadership within the existing rubrics.[2]

- Several "new style denominations" (they would resist that label) have come into being as the result of the expansion of independent congregations that grew out of the 1960s

counterculture: congregations networked as part of the
Vineyard Christian Fellowship and the Calvary Chapel
and Grace Chapel movements.[3] These networks of congregations look to a "mother" church that has spawned
them for guidance, resources, and sometimes discipline.[4]
Similarly, the Willow Creek Association, while not a denomination, functions as one in defining a particular ecclesial style, providing resources for churches that would
become "seeker" churches, providing training for staff,
and organizing communications networks among member congregations.

I do not pretend to treat all of these new ecclesial forms in what follows. I mention the longer list because the examples challenge us to reflect on them and what they represent. If one is a legalist about denominationally prescribed ecclesial patterns, then she or he may find some
of these developments disconcerting if not disheartening. If, however,
one believes, as I do, that they are signs of a healthy, if sometimes
painful, ferment in ecclesiology that often originates at the local level,
then one may take heart and find in them some clues to renewal and vitality. I suggest that we think of them as "local ecclesiologies," ecclesial parallels to what Robert Schreiter (1985) called "local theologies."
In *Constructing Local Theologies,* Schreiter's concern was not with
academic theology undertaken by professional theologians but with the
theology to which local communities of faith give expression. A local
theology is constructed or emerges, he suggests, where a local church
or community encounters the gospel in the context of its particular culture. Congregations and other communities of faith construct local theologies as they wrestle with how they are to be faithful to the gospel and
to received traditions of Christian faith within the concrete situations
and cultural contexts in which they find themselves. Local theologies
are not inferior to academic theologies; they are simply different. Similarly "local ecclesiologies" are *organizational forms and practices
through which local congregations attempt to give expression to the
gospel and received ecclesial traditions in ways appropriate to their local social and cultural contexts.*
Ecclesiology is that branch of theology that deals with the nature,
constitution, and functions of the church. It deals with such things as
structures of authority, roles, liturgical practices (including music), organizational patterns, decision making, and the like—ways in which
congregations should be organized to give expression to their mission.

As with theology generally, we have academic ecclesiologies, and we have official denominational ecclesiologies that are spelled out, for example, in the Presbyterian Church's *Book of Order* or the Methodist's *Book of Discipline*. We also know, however, that local congregations often embody not only the official ecclesiological pattern but also their own variations of it. Furthermore, as the examples I cited illustrate, some of the newer ecclesial forms break with received traditions and attempt new forms of church life and practice.

One need not agree with or accept uncritically all that these and other developments imply, but it is crucial that we try to understand and learn from them as we attempt to order our congregational life for faithful ministry in a new millennium. In their book on mainline Protestant renewal, Joseph Coalter, John Mulder, and Lewis Weeks (1996: 59) call for a rebuilding of what they label Protestant ecosystems: "those institutions and practices—both formal and informal—which [have] undergirded Christian commitment and faith." Among the ecosystems that they discuss, none is more important than local congregations and their practices. As they say (81–82), "Religious vitality exists primarily in local congregations. Any rebuilding of ecosystems of nurture must therefore focus on congregations."

The focus on congregations—especially on these emerging new local ecclesial forms and practices—is my concern. Unlike Bellamy a century ago, I will not try to forecast what new congregational forms will emerge in the coming century. Indeed, as I will make clear, it is impossible to do so. The pace of change will no doubt lead us to experience a variety of new congregational forms in the twenty-first century. Thus rather than play the prophet, I attempt instead to address the following questions: What lies behind these emerging ecclesial forms and practices? How can we try to make sense of them? How do we "test their spirits"? Have they any lessons for mainline Protestants and other mainline traditions as we try to rebuild ecosystems of faith?

In chapter 1, I review changes in patterns of congregational life in America as a reminder that experiencing innovations in congregational life is nothing new, not in the broad sweep of Christian history and especially not in the American experience. Despite this, the innovations we are witnessing today are unusual in their scope and direction. Why is this so? I propose that we understand them as responses to what I call a posttraditional world, the basic characteristics of which I try to describe. In the second chapter, I analyze in greater detail several of the previously mentioned innovative ecclesial forms that, I maintain, reflect different types of responses to a posttraditional world. I pay special attention to some of the new style or posttraditional congregations—for example, those that are also called seeker or mall-type churches. In the third chapter, I consider theological issues raised by these new ecclesial forms, especially the age-old tension between tradition and freedom. I find it particularly helpful to see how this tension played itself out in New Testament churches and various other moments of Christian history and ask how it is instructive for us today. I also propose norms for evaluating such responses. Finally, I focus on some of the lessons that we can learn from these various newer local ecclesial forms, especially the new style or posttraditional churches. I do not argue that we should emulate them uncritically, but I am convinced that we have much to learn from them as we shape our congregations to meet the challenges of a new millennium.

Earlier versions of these chapters were presented as public lectures. They were initially delivered as the Sprunt Lectures at Union Theological Seminary in Virginia in 1997. Also in 1997, I had the privilege of presenting a shortened and revised version of the lectures to groups of pastors and laypersons at three locations in South Africa, under the auspices of the University of Stellenbosch. The lectures, further revised, were presented as the Smythe Lectures at Columbia Theological Seminary, Decatur, Georgia, in 1998. I am deeply grateful to these three institutions for making it possible for me to present the lectures and for their hospitality. I especially appreciate the many thoughtful conversations with those who heard them and offered constructive feedback. I am also grateful to my wife, Anne Ewing Carroll, who gave her usual helpful critique and loving support during the preparation of the lectures and endured hearing them on more than one occasion.

On the dedication page, I have listed the names of our six grandchildren. I dedicate the book to them, not only to honor them and express my love and appreciation for the joy they bring; but I also pray that as they inhabit the new century they will find healthy, vital congregations that will nurture and deepen their faith and provide them with opportunities to participate in God's ongoing work in the world.

1

Changing Society,
Changing Churches

> To the distinctiveness of its calling and commission, and therefore to the form of its existence as the people of God in [the] world . . . , there does not correspond in the first instance or intrinsically any absolutely distinctive social form [of the church].
>
> *Karl Barth (1962: 739)*

Unlike sermons, books do not typically have texts; yet this one does. It comes from a passage in Karl Barth's *Church Dogmatics,* from which the above epigraph is taken. Affirming that the church's existence depends solely on its calling by Jesus Christ, Barth not only argues against any intrinsic or distinctive social form that the church must take, but he also continues:

> Notwithstanding peculiarities in detail, in every age and place its constitution and order have been broadly determined and conditioned by political, economic, and cultural models more or less imperatively forced on it by its situation in world history. . . . It has had and still has to adapt or approximate itself to these in order to maintain itself, or, no less subject to the law of its environment, it has had and still has to evade or oppose them in respect of the form of its existence. . . . Either way, . . . there has never been anywhere . . . an intrinsically sacred sociology [of the church]. Obviously there is no such thing, just as there is no absolutely distinctive or intrinsically sacred language. In this respect . . . the people of God exists in worldly fashion within [the] world.

Barth's words may be difficult for "polity purists" to swallow. The "sociologies" of our denominations' manuals of church order are, for some, more sacred than the Bible! But I ask the reader to try to suspend judgment about these sacred sociologies and hang on instead to the implication of Barth's words that many of the current ecclesial changes need not be life threatening. The church has been through change before—"it's been there and done that"—and has found the grace to respond to changes in ways that have been creative in their various contexts and faithful to the gospel. *"There has never been anywhere . . . an intrinsically sacred sociology [of the church]."*

Ecclesial Patterns in the United States

I will have more to say in later chapters about other implications of Barth's perspective for understanding and assessing new ecclesial forms. For the present, however, note his contention that "in every age and place the church's constitution and order have been broadly determined and conditioned by political, economic, and cultural models more or less imperatively forced on it by its situation in world history." This does not necessarily mean that ecclesial patterns are *only* a reflection of their times, but rather that as church leaders have sought to achieve the church's purposes, they have often adapted ecclesial forms, wittingly or unwittingly, from dominant models in the broader political, economic, and cultural scene, especially those that have appeared to be successful. Craig Dykstra and James Hudnut-Beumler (1992) provide an example of how this has been so for denominational organizations in the United States. They describe how American denominations evolved in relation to larger cultural models: first as "voluntary societies" organized to accomplish some larger mission beyond the capacities of local congregations; then as "corporate denominations," emulating the giant corporate structures emerging elsewhere in business and government; and currently in their role as "regulatory agencies" for congregational practices, not unlike the way that many governmental regulatory agencies function in relation to other areas of social, economic, and political life. In each case, denominational patterns to some degree mimicked the influence of the larger cultural patterns.

"We've Always Done It This Way"—Or Have We?

Especially pertinent to my concern with congregational forms and practices in this book, historian Brooks Holifield (1994) has traced the history of American congregational models, considering various ways that they have changed over the course of American history. His analysis not only confirms Barth's point that there is no sacred sociology of the church, but it can also aid our reflections about our own situation. It is helpful to highlight briefly Holifield's major points, especially with regard to Protestant congregations. He traces the evolution of congregations through four models, the residues of which continue to be visible in present congregational forms.

The earliest model was dominant in the period from the early settlement of America to roughly the establishment of the republic at the end of the eighteenth century. During this period, American communities were quite small, and the dominant congregational model was what Holifield calls the *comprehensive congregation,* so named because the ideal was only one congregation per community, one that would comprehend the entire community. Conducting public worship was the congregation's reason for being. There was no Sunday school or other church organizations as we know them. When there were church fights, the fights were usually over issues of worship: who takes Communion, who gets baptized and how, and should the congregation sing hymns? If so, how? Lay control was strong—so strong that clergy began to form ministerial associations to gain greater ministerial authority over congregations. Comprehensive congregations were public institutions with a strong sense of communal responsibility. Not only did they provide aid for the poor, but they often exercised discipline for everything from drunkenness and fornication to shoddy business dealings.

Comprehensive congregations gave way to a second model, the *devotional congregation,* which was the dominant model until shortly after the Civil War. This type of congregation reflected the growing diversity of American life. Towns expanded in size and developed segmented patterns of work and social life that were quite different from those of small villages and rural areas. Social class and racial distinctions became more prominent. The impact of the Great Awakening was especially significant, bringing with it a proliferation of congregations as Baptists and Methodists, in particular, evangelized the countryside. Now a town may not have had just one congregation but several, and they competed with one another for members. These congregations developed a variety of new patterns that reflected the growing segmentation of social life: Sunday schools, prayer meetings, Bible classes, and mission societies. Worship styles also proliferated, especially as the democratizing rhetoric of the era encouraged rejection of the "refined sermons and dignified prayers" of the older traditions. As Holifield (1994: 35) notes, "The groups that grew fastest incorporated gospel hymns sung to popular

tunes, loud and exuberant shouting, and colorful colloquial preaching."
All this was in contrast to the services of the more fashionable urban
churches of the day with their organs, professional singers, and educated
clergy.

Most of these devotional congregations changed little as the nineteenth century came to a close. Indeed, many congregations today, especially small congregations in rural areas and small towns, continue to
exhibit the devotional pattern. In the larger urban areas, however, as
diversity increased and urban life became even more segmented, a new
model emerged: what Holifield calls the *social congregation*. Noting that
Catholic parishes were—to use current parlance—"seven-day-a-week"
institutions, Protestants also transformed their congregations "into cen-
ters that not only were open for worship but also were available for Sunday school concerts, church socials, women's meetings, youth groups,
girls' guilds, boys' brigades, sewing circles, benevolent societies, day
schools, temperance societies, athletic clubs, scout troops, and nameless
other activities" (Holifield 1994: 39–40). Worship took a different turn
in these social congregations: strong preaching continued to be emphasized, but there was more congregational singing and prayers and
responsive readings. Beyond their walls, these congregations engaged in
extensive social ministries. Calling themselves "institutional churches,"
they built gymnasiums, schools, and boarding houses for single women;
and they established libraries, clinics, clubs, and classes for the tenement
dwellers in the surrounding neighborhoods.

Holifield's final type, what he calls the *participatory congregation*,
brings us to the present. With roots in the earlier social model but also
reflecting life since the 1950s, participatory congregations offer the
broad range of programs and groups that characterized social congregations. These programs, however, are designed to address the needs of
a more diverse laity who are much more self-conscious about their
involvement, picking and choosing what parts of the church's life will
claim their attention and resisting or rejecting that which does not meet
their needs or interests. Architectural styles reflect the changes, with
worship spaces designed to permit congregations to act together litur-
gically rather than witness a "performance" put on by clergy and paid
musicians. While Holifield does not discuss it, worship styles have also
evolved and become increasingly diverse in participatory congregations.[1] On the one hand, there is the recent liturgical renewal that has cut
across various denominational lines and emphasizes a recovery of classical traditions of worship that are, in fact, participatory in style. On the
other hand, there are the much more contemporary and informal wor-

ship styles, especially those that involve considerable congregational singing of praise choruses and use of multimedia presentations. In the next chapter, I consider these changing worship styles and a number of other characteristics of a particular variety of participatory congregations that I call posttraditional congregations.

The important point to be gleaned from this excursus into the history of American congregational forms and practices is a reinforcement of Barth's words that there is no "intrinsically sacred sociology [of the church]." Our present-day churches reflect a variety of local ecclesial forms and practices, many of which have come to us out of our past and others that are evolving in response to current changes in the broader culture and society. Moreover, as Barth notes, in every age they reflect patterns or models adapted from the larger culture.

Additional Influences on Congregational Diversity

Several other points about current congregational patterns and practices are worth noting here. Although Holifield takes into account denominational variations within his types, and although such variations continue to be pertinent, denominationally distinct ecclesial forms are of less and less importance. Across denominations, including even some Catholic parishes, we are witnessing considerable blurring of denominational distinctives as congregations borrow from one another in their ecclesial practices. In some cases this is the result of ecumenical contact and cooperation over the past half century or more. Churches have worked together to forge common patterns for doing things. In worship, for example, the ecumenical liturgical renewal movement that I mentioned previously has played an important role in efforts to recover or develop new common worship forms. Worship in many Methodist or Presbyterian church services, often using the Word and Table liturgical format, are surprisingly similar to those one might experience in a Catholic or Episcopal or Lutheran parish. Theological understandings that lie behind sacramental observances may differ, but many of the liturgical forms are comparable.

Another major reason for the similarity among congregations across denominational lines is the growth of localism in congregational life. Increasingly local concerns take precedence over those of the denomination. Local leaders and members determine how they will function and what ministries they will engage in, even when their decisions contravene denominational directives or priorities. The result is a "de facto congregationalism."[2] Regardless of their denomination's polity, whether it is hierarchical, connectional, or congregational, many congregations are essentially voluntary gathered communities, following more or less the pattern of the Reformed church tradition. De facto congregationalism does not, however, lead to "a thousand flowers blooming," or more literally to 350,000 (the estimated number of congregations in the United States), with each congregation staking out a markedly different pattern from all the others. Rather, congregations borrow from one another across denominational lines and even across faith traditions. Muslims and Buddhists, for example, have developed congregational patterns as they have settled in the United States that are in many ways quite alien to their traditions in their lands of origin but quite similar to those developed by the Protestant Christian majority. Their leaders have thought that such borrowing is necessary if they are to be considered legitimate players in America's religious milieu.

In other cases of borrowing across denominational lines, it is primarily a matter of copying or adapting practices that have succeeded in another congregation. The ecclesial environment is highly uncertain, and membership declines among many congregations, especially in mainline Protestant denominations, have created considerable anxiety and a search for congregational models that appear successful. Books, clergy journals, workshops, consultants, and even the Internet regularly describe successful innovations. The most widely known success story is that of Willow Creek Community Church, one of the congregations that I call posttraditional. It is no surprise that Willow Creek's seeker service and small-group ministry have been widely imitated by mainline as well as evangelical congregations. A growing number of congregations have discarded many of their inherited traditions of worship and church programming in favor of adapting Willow Creek's innovative practices to their own settings. They have also followed Willow Creek in borrowing marketing strategies from the business world to identify and attract potential constituents.

If, however, they borrow from one another across denominational lines or from secular sources, many congregations, as a result of local autonomy, often try to stake out their distinctiveness as they compete with one another at the local level for new members, resources, and the voluntary commitment of existing members. Such "niche" congregations—somewhat on the analogy of boutiques—may include ones that specialize in a ministry to gays and lesbians, while others may design their congregation's programs and practices to minister to deaf persons or to those with other challenges. Others aim at attracting a particular generational group—for example, Baby Boomers or members of Generation X. Others serve particular ethnic communities, while yet others define their niche in terms of an outstanding music or educational program. One United Methodist congregation in Virginia has developed its niche around an animal ministry. The pastor, a former circus animal trainer, keeps various live animals on a nearby farm and uses them during worship services and on other occasions as aids to his preaching and teaching. Many Catholic parishes and large Protestant congregations often develop a variety of worship services and programs, each different in character and each designed to appeal to a particular "market" segment. In many niche congregations inherited denominational traditions or ecclesial patterns do not play a primary role.

The use of market language to describe what is happening with congregations is frequently resisted by religious leaders, often for good reasons. It does, however, provide important insights into what has happened to congregations and denominations in the past, and it also illumines the current fluid scene that I am trying to interpret. Indeed, the usefulness of market language for understanding American religion has led some historians and sociologists to adopt what has come to be called "the religious economies perspective" (Hatch 1989; Finke and Stark 1992; Warner 1993; Moore 1994).[3] Religious institutions in the United States operate within an open religious market in contrast to the monopolistic situation of countries with an established religion. Such an open market makes possible religious pluralism with a minimum of conflict. It also makes individual choice in religious participation a major feature of American religious life, a matter to which I return in the next chapter.

In short, then, congregational patterns and practices have not only varied considerably over time, as Holifield's analysis shows, but they also differ substantially at any given time. These differences are less and less dictated by denominational distinctives; rather, they are influenced by local circumstances, de facto congregationalism, borrowing models that others have found to be successful, and competition in the religious marketplace.[4] It is often easy to forget this variability, especially when someone—perhaps a new pastor—attempts to change some cherished congregational practice and hears the familiar refrain: "We've always done it this way!" This statement is often not simply a statement of fact but also a warning: "Don't dare try to change things if you know what is good for you!" Yet things have not always been done the same way; existing patterns are not sacrosanct; and acknowledging this point need not be experienced as threatening. It can be liberating as it frees us to ask how, as we face new challenges, God is calling us to be faithful as Christ's body in the world.

Acknowledging the diversity of church forms from the past also raises other important questions. What is driving the present shift to participatory congregations? Why have we developed a de facto congregationalism that cuts across denominational and religious traditions in the United States? Why are we experiencing the emergence today of innovative new ecclesial forms?

Whatever Happened to Tradition?

In large measure, the changes that are taking place in church life are related to much broader social and cultural shifts that have been underway, first in the West and now globally. I examine some of the ecclesial changes themselves in the following chapter; it will help in understanding them to examine here some of the key shifts that are occurring. Analysts have used a variety of categories to try to understand these shifts.

Secularization has long been the favorite explanatory concept, but increasingly it has come under criticism for its limitations, in part because it has been used with no clear or consistent meaning and also because it does not always square with actual changes that we can observe.[5] Among other meanings, secularization has typically been used to imply sharp declines in religious belief and practice, especially as compared with a former age of faith—Christendom in the Middle Ages, for example. In the United States an idealized version of a deeply Christian, Puritan New England is often used as the touchstone for measuring decline. Some secularization theorists have assumed the eventual demise of religious institutions and even of religion itself except as an extremely private, marginal, and "invisible" phenomenon (e.g., Luckmann 1967).

Secularization as religious decline works reasonably well as an explanation of what is happening in established (state) churches in western Europe, but unless secularization is quite carefully defined, it has limited usefulness for interpreting the religious scene in the United States and especially in Third World societies. With reference to American religion, it is true that we have experienced significant religious change in recent years, and a number of religious institutions and practices have undergone decline or near extinction. Yet to explain all such changes as secularization—meaning the decline and eventual demise of religion—is inadequate if not wrong. There is too much religious ferment both inside and outside the churches for secularization to be an adequate explanation. The various new ecclesial forms to which I called attention in the introduction are examples of the ferment. One of the staunchest advocates of secularization theory, sociologist Peter Berger, has acknowledged that its application to the United States and many non-Western societies was a mistake. "Modernity, as has become increasingly clear, is not necessarily linked to secularization. It is so in a few areas of the world, notably in Western Europe, and in some internationally visible groups, notably the humanistically educated intelligentsia. Most of the world today is as religious as it ever was and, in a good many locales, more religious than ever" (Berger 1998: 782).

Posttraditional Society?

Acknowledging the limits of secularization theories to explain the social and cultural shifts that are driving current religious change, others have sought alternative explanatory frameworks, for example, one or another of various "posts-": *post*industrial, *post*-Christian, *post*liberal, *post*-Protestant, *post*materialist, and a current favorite, *post*modern—to say what is happening. Each of these has been helpful in interpreting some aspect of the changes that the user has wished to explain, but each has its limitations and its critics. Instead of using one of these categories or summarizing their various critics, I add to the list with yet another "post-": post*traditional*.

I use "posttraditional" rather than, for example, the closely related term, "postmodern," not simply because the latter, like "secularization," has become ideologically loaded without a clearly agreed upon meaning, but because I believe "posttraditional" better addresses the issues with which I am concerned in this book.[6] Although the term "posttraditional" has its own limitations, it is especially helpful in understanding the kinds of ecclesial changes that are my concern. Most of the changes in church life are in large measure challenges to time-honored traditions, for example, traditional liturgical patterns, traditional hymns, traditional musical instruments such as the pipe organ, traditional church architecture, traditional organizational patterns. Even in cases where our received traditions are being reclaimed, they are not left untouched but are being reshaped in light of new understandings and experiences.

But the use of "posttraditional" to describe what is taking place has its problems. The various "posts-," including posttraditional, suggest a bipolar view of society: there was once one kind of society, but now we have moved beyond it. We are now postindustrial, postmodern, posttraditional, and so on. Reality, however, does not divide so neatly. Society is not dichotomous, and bipolar views exclude important middle terms. History is much more complex, rarely moving in such a linear, clear-cut fashion. Yet, if one takes "posttraditional" as denoting not a finished state but a process that involves major social and cultural shifts that have profound implications for cherished traditions, then I find it a helpful term. It implies that something has occurred or is occurring in Western—and in many cases global—society that is transforming previously taken-for-granted social and cultural patterns, including ecclesial traditions.

Another similar way of describing what is happening that connotes more of a process than posttraditional implies is to speak of *detraditionalization*, which is the title of a recent collection of essays (Heelas, Lash, and Morris 1996). We may not yet be completely posttraditional, but we are experiencing detraditionalization. We are not *beyond* tradition; nonetheless, we have moved to a place where inherited traditions play less and less decisive roles in the way that we understand and order our lives, including our ecclesial forms and practices. Or they play quite different roles than they have played in the past. If traditions remain important to us, they do so because we *choose* to follow them; we *choose* to acknowledge their importance; we *choose* to seek their guidance in the changed and changing contexts in which we live. And we often reinterpret and change them in the process. Such responses to tradition are quite different from the kind of inevitable, taken-for-granted way that individuals in most societies have experienced traditions in the past.

Traditions and Their Importance

Before I pursue further what detraditionalization means and what is driving it, it will help to reflect briefly on the meaning and role of tradition generally and especially with respect to religion. "Tradition," from the Latin root *tradere* (to hand over or entrust), refers generally to the collective memory of a particular group through which it passes on its accrued wisdom, gained through facing various challenges, perils, and uncertainties of life, including both small challenges of day-to-day living as well as big questions of life and death. Although a group's tradition addresses themes and concerns of everyday, profane life, it also includes sacred lore—wisdom having to do with the group's relationship to the sacred—which signals the tradition's normative character. The tradition's collective wisdom is expressed in stories, songs, beliefs, and precepts; it is enacted in rituals and ceremonies; and it is passed from generation to generation.

In this connection two other Latin terms are useful: *traditum* and *traditio*. The former refers to the core "deposit" of the collective memory, while the latter refers to the core's various adaptations as it is handed down from generation to generation and in new and different sociocultural contexts to which the original deposit must speak.[7] In the United States, the *traditum* could perhaps be thought of as the core set of beliefs and values captured in the Declaration of Independence and the Constitution. These core values are celebrated in myths, symbols, and rituals (stories of the Pilgrims, founding fathers, and heroes; symbols such as a "city set on a hill" or the Statue of Liberty; and rituals such as those surrounding Memorial Day, July Fourth, and Thanksgiving). Adaptations of the core—the *traditum*—are numerous and disparate in various periods of American history: the settlement of the West, responses to slavery such as that of the abolitionists, the doctrine of Manifest Destiny, the Civil Rights struggles of the 1950s and 1960s, or the rhetoric and work of the Religious Right in the present. This distinction is also useful in discussion of the church's tradition(s), both *traditio* and *traditum*; but I reserve this discussion until chapter 3. For now, instead, let us consider other characteristics and functions of tradition, including its relation to individuals.

As individuals, each of us has our own particular story, our own particular way of being in the world and responding to its challenges, that unfolds from our birth to our death and expresses our identity. But our individual stories are not simply individual or self-contained. They are part of the larger narratives or traditions (both *traditio* and *traditum)* in which we participate by virtue of our parents, extended family, and religion. We also participate in the stories and traditions of our community, region, and nation. These larger narratives of family, society, and religion may form a seamless whole, as in relatively simple or isolated societies. As society becomes more complex, however, we may find ourselves to be part of multiple, even conflicting stories and traditions (including both *traditio* and *traditum*) that make it necessary to choose which will have priority in our lives, or, instead, which will have priority at given times and places in our lives.

We learn about tradition(s) from our elders—parents, teachers, and leaders, including religious leaders—as they tell the stories and interpret and reinterpret them for the present. We learn them in particular from observing our elders' behavior in their practices, especially in rituals that enact the stories and meanings of the collective memory and also connect them to the present. More than simply recounting the tradition, as sociologist Anthony Giddens says, "ritual firmly connects the ritual reconstruction of the past with practical enactment [in the present] and can be seen to do so" (1994: 64).

In his autobiography, Nelson Mandela (1994: 11) describes the processes through which he learned African traditions, especially of his Xhosa tribe, and also Christian traditions:

> Like all Xhosa children, I acquired knowledge mainly through observation. We were meant to learn through imitation and emulation, not through questions. When I first visited whites, I was often dumbfounded by the number and nature of questions that children asked of their parents—and their parents' unfailing willingness to answer them. In my household, questions were considered a nuisance; adults imparted information as they considered necessary.
>
> My life, and that of most Xhosas at the time, was shaped by custom, ritual, and taboo. This was the alpha and omega of our existence, and went unquestioned. Men followed the path laid out for them by their fathers; women led the same lives as their mothers had before them.

Mandela also tells of the impact on him of the stories he heard from chiefs and elders who gathered regularly at the home of a leading chief where he lived as a young teenager, and of the respect and awe in which he held the local Methodist pastor, whose "powerful presence embodied all that was alluring in Christianity" (19).

What do traditions do? Why are they important? We can consider these questions from the standpoint of both the individual and the group or community. I have already hinted at some of the answers.

From the individual's perspective, one function of traditions is to help one locate oneself in the larger narratives of family, tribe, or community. Traditions provide a "genealogy," real or imagined (Hervieu-Léger 1994), that connects individuals with ancestors, contemporaries, and successors. In these narratives, we are given an identity: Xhosa, not Zulu; Hispanic, not Anglo; Protestant, not Catholic; Presbyterian, not Baptist; North American, not European; and so on.

Second, traditions provide us with the basic frames or perspectives through which we view the world. Although we are usually unaware of this interpretive role of traditions, as similarly we are most of the time unaware of the air we breathe, our traditions supply the beliefs, stories, symbols (including language), and categories by which we frame our experiences of the world and make sense of things. As the American poet Wallace Stevens suggests in one of his poems, we live in the description of a place and not in the place itself.[8] Our traditions supply the categories for the description. In this sense, we cannot finally speak of detraditionalization as if it meant getting rid of this interpretive role of traditions. Even as older interpretive traditions are undermined, new ones—though perhaps less coherent than the old—take their place.

Third, traditions help us to learn what is expected of us, in a general sense, both in day-to-day routines and in relationships with others. They not only help us decide what is the good for us individually in this or that circumstance, but they also put the question in a larger context of the good for our family, community, nation, fellow human beings, or the environment. All of this we learn as a kind of recipe-like knowledge that we accept more or less without question—at least until, like Nelson Mandela, we experience other ways of doing things that make us stop and think.

Finally, because traditions connect us with larger narratives from the past in which we can locate ourselves, and because they also give us perspectives and precepts that guide our understanding and behavior in the present, they also to some degree shape how we organize our future. This is especially applicable when we live in relatively settled times. The future can be reasonably faced and organized in terms of what we have known and done in the past.

In considering the role of traditions, let me note especially the importance of religious traditions. Religious traditions locate us with reference not only to our family and other human communities but also to the sacred. My identity is given sacred meaning. I am not only a member of this or that family and community, but I am also a child of God, made in God's image, loved by God, called to understand the world and to live according to God's purposes. I am also helped to see and interpret my experiences and actions in light of the sacred stories and meanings embodied in the traditions and practices of my community of fellow believers. For Christians, baptism is the sacrament that gives sacred meaning to our identity. We are given both a Christian name and membership in a new extended family, the people of God. Further, our identity is rehearsed and renewed in practices of worship, including especially Communion or the Eucharist.

But it is not only my identity that is given sacred meaning. The interpretive frameworks and the prescriptions for living also take on a normative, often sacred, character. They are not simply valuable wisdom from the past that we can take or leave; they are believed to be divinely ordained. Roman Catholics, for example, express this in the doctrine of papal infallibility. Some Protestants do so similarly in the belief in the absolute authority of an infallible, even inerrant, scripture.

Traditions also play similar and important roles for groups, including religious communities such as denominations and congregations.

As with individuals, they give groups particular identities, shape their perspectives, define their boundaries, guide their behavior, and help them to organize themselves for action in the world about them. For example, Presbyterians have the Reformed tradition, expressed in stories about John Calvin, John Knox, and other Reformed worthies; in teachings such as Calvin's *Institutes*; in various historic confessions; in the *Book of Order*; and in time-honored ecclesial practices and moral and spiritual disciplines that have a distinctly Reformed flavor. Likewise Methodism, the denominational narrative in which I locate myself, has its Wesleyan heritage, embodied not only in John Wesley's writings and personal example, but also in Charles Wesley's hymns, in Francis Asbury's circuit-riding ministry, and especially in the Methodist *Book of Discipline,* which lays out specific guidelines for polity and practice. Presbyterians, Methodists, and other denominations are also inheritors of the catholic Christian tradition, which links us, more or less, across confessional boundaries. Similarly, every local congregation that has been in existence for much time at all has its own local traditions that often take on almost sacred status—stories out of the congregation's past, memories of particular "church mothers" and "fathers," beliefs, customs, and practices peculiar to the congregation.

Because traditions are typically widely accepted—taken for granted in many cases—they have a heavy emotional and moral content that is given added weight by their special connection with the sacred. That is why they are so hard to change or ignore and why we often encounter severe conflicts (both externally and internally) when we do try to change them. A standing joke within Eastern Orthodoxy is that some things change quickly; others take more time: short-term changes take about four hundred years! At the same time, however, traditions are not static. Unless they are dead traditions, they are dynamic, changing, always in the process of being interpreted and adapted to meet new circumstances (as implied in the word *traditio*). In his book *After Virtue,* the philosopher Aladair MacIntyre (1984: 221–22) maintains that living traditions always embody continuous arguments about what it means to live by them: what it means to be a good citizen or a good community or a good Lutheran congregation, for example. Such arguments involve continuing conflicts as we engage in traditioning or retraditioning, adapting traditions to changing circumstances, even if at times we pretend that nothing has really changed.

This last point is especially important. I emphasize it here and will return to it in subsequent chapters. Honoring one's tradition does not mean having an antiquarian interest in one's past. One does not honor tradition simply because it is old. Honoring tradition is not a call to carry forward, reenact, repristinate, or imitate some pattern or precept just as it was done in the past (or just because it was done in the past). Instead, as MacIntyre implies, one argues with one's tradition, adapts it to one's new circumstances. As one does so, the tradition does not remain static but changes too. That is what makes it a living body of collective wisdom.

I have portrayed the consequences of tradition in mostly positive terms. It is clear, however, that traditions also have their shadow side. Individuals and groups can become so rooted in traditional ways of perceiving the world and behaving that they are unable to adapt to new circumstances. Their practices from the past cease to be living traditions. Traditions can also lead groups to establish such high boundaries that they cannot coexist with others whose identity is found in different narratives. The last result is painfully and tragically evident in the continuing legacy of racism in this country; in the multiethnic, multireligious strife that we have witnessed in Bosnia and Kosovo; in the hostilities between Catholics and Protestants in Northern Ireland; in the struggle between Palestinian Arabs (Muslims and Christians) and Jews in the Holy Land; or in tribal genocide in Rwanda, to take but a few current examples. In these and other cases, traditions and the boundaries they establish have become rigid and fixed, so much so that the group is unable to ask the question of the "good" in any broader sense than its own self-interest. Although these examples take us far beyond the question of posttraditional ecclesial responses that are the concern of these chapters, the negative consequences of an unbending commitment to traditional beliefs and practices and an unwillingness to entertain change are evident in the large and small conflicts that occupy church leaders as they encounter detraditionalizing processes.

Detraditionalization

To say that we live in a posttraditional or detraditionalizing society is not to say that traditions are no longer important or operative in our lives. It is rather to say that something important is happening to the way that we relate to traditions, including religious traditions. For an increasing number of people, many traditions no longer carry the authoritative weight they once did. For some, they carry no weight at all; they are relics of a dead past. In one sense, this rejection of tradition is nothing new. Although it has its roots even earlier,[9] the attack on tradition was especially intense in the eighteenth-century Enlightenment with its emphasis on reason and the autonomous individual, free from the tyranny of tradition. Anthony Giddens (1994: 93) maintains, however, that modernity (what is sometimes called the Enlightenment Project) only appeared to be antitraditional. It was really about building new traditions even as it was dissolving old ones: for example, the legitimacy of the state's power over its subjects, the primacy of reason and scientific knowledge, the rights of individuals, and a belief in inevitable progress through science and technology. Living in a university community as I do, one quickly encounters the continuing power of these Enlightenment-inspired traditions when one questions the all-sufficiency of reason or suggests that there are experiences that science cannot ultimately explain. Furthermore, for quite a long period, modernity left some older traditions relatively untouched: the family, for example,[10] or more traditional definitions of sexual identity. Also, so long as we identified "modern" with the West, we often failed to notice the continuing power of tradition in other areas of the globe. Now, however, we are in transition globally to a posttraditional society. No society is untouched. Detraditionalizing processes affect us all and call to account the unquestioned authority of both ancient and modern traditions. To use the pregnant phrase of Jean-François Lyotard, one of the French apostles of postmodernism, we have witnessed "the end of the grand narratives," including especially those that were the creations of modernity (Lyotard 1984).[11]

At its heart then, posttraditional society and detraditionalization are about changing conceptions of authority and truth. At the risk of overstatement, I will put it as sharply as possible: Detraditionalization is a process that involves a shift of authority from something that is "out there" and external to us—for example, an inherited way of life, an inerrant scripture, an infallible teaching office, one of the historic confessions, or the Enlightenment's traditions of the primacy of science and progress—to authority that resides "in here," in the self, in the authority of our own knowledge and experience as individuals. No longer do we rely without question on traditional formulae for doing things or on the power of long-established institutions and their representatives to give us directives for living; rather, we are often thrown back on ourselves and our own experience to find appropriate ways to respond to challenges that arise in our lives. "'Voice' is displaced from established sources, coming to rest with the self" (Heelas, Lash, and Morris 1996: 2). As a result, we are now compelled to live *reflexively* or *reflectively*,[12] both personally and, in terms of the focus of this book, ecclesially. To live reflexively does not require abandoning one's traditions; instead it means not trusting or following them uncritically—neither the wisdom of the past nor the newer traditions of scientific-instrumental modes of thought. It involves testing received wisdom by personal experience, by one's own frame of reference, as well as by new knowledge as we reflect critically on the choices that confront us. It involves willingness to engage in dialogue with other traditions and alternative ways of doing things.

In sum, individuals in traditional societies have found direction for their lives, limits placed on their choices, and identities that are preassigned or ascribed by the communities into which they are born. In a detraditionalized world, in contrast, we are confronted daily with a multitude of choices that cause us to live reflexively, constructing our own identities as posttraditional people. No single, uncontested tradition provides a secure and seamless narrative framework for our lives. Instead, "the question, 'How shall I live?' has to be answered in day-to-day decisions about how to behave, what to wear, what to eat—and many other things—as well as interpreted with the temporal unfolding of self-identity" (Giddens 1991: 14). And what is true for these day-to-day decisions is also true religiously. A sociologist friend from Belgium (Dobbelaere 1991) illustrates this in the story of a Catholic couple in a catechism class who asked their priest whether it was alright for the wife to use the pill. "Ask them," the priest said, pointing to other lay members in the discussion group. "If you ask me publicly, I will have to say no. So don't ask me. Discuss it among yourselves." In other words, make your decision reflexively.

In a more general way, we Americans illustrate detraditionalization in the way that we identify ourselves religiously. We refer to having a religious *preference*. "I happen to be a Lutheran" or "I happen to be a Baptist."[13] Such expressions would make no sense in a traditional society where religious identities are ascribed, where one is born into a religious identity.

It is these changes, characteristic of posttraditional society, that are not only affecting individual identity construction and decision making but also contributing to the experimentation and change in ecclesial forms and practices.

Forces Driving Detraditionalization

We can understand something of what is driving detraditionalization by considering how traditions are sustained. As MacIntyre maintains (1984: 263), traditions must be socially embodied if they are to be living traditions. That is, traditions must be incarnated, given institutional expression, and practiced in communities, especially face-to-face communities such as homes, congregations, schools, and neighborhoods.

Earlier I referred to such communities as "ecosystems" for nurturing faith. We can also think of them as "institutions of memory" (Hervieu-Léger 1994) that keep alive a people's stories. It is in such communities, with their practices and the networks of friends, family members, and authoritative teachers (guardians of the tradition), that individuals throughout history have learned the traditions of their community, including their religious faith. And it is in these ecosystems that they have found social support and encouragement to live by them. Even great transnational traditions, like those of the church, must find local embodiment where they can be practiced if they are to shape our lives and our identities, if they are to connect us to a shared past, form us in the present, and influence the ways that we organize the future.

Although this may seem self-evident, what has happened is that the social relations that have supported the passing on of traditions have undergone profound changes. They have become *disembedded,* to use Giddens's (1991) helpful term. That is, many of our day-to-day social relationships have been lifted out of the time- and place-bound local contexts and communities in which traditions and tradition-bearing institutions have had their powerful identity-shaping effects.[14] Destabilizing these social relationships likewise destabilizes the traditions that they embody and the practices that sustain the traditions.[15] Their authority over us is weakened, and we are thrown back reflexively on the authority of our own experience to make the multiple choices that are open to us. Increasingly, one's identity becomes self-authored rather than bestowed by circumstances of one's birth, family, community, or nation.

Whereas disembedding processes have rapidly accelerated in recent years, especially since the 1960s, such processes have been occurring at least since the time of the Protestant Reformation. The Reformers were early detraditionalizers who played important roles in fostering the shift to modernity and to posttraditional society. This was especially true of John Calvin and his followers. Calvinist Protestants were disembedded individuals, part of an emerging urban middle class who left traditional village communities to make their way in commerce in the cities that were coming into existence throughout Europe. The Reformers' teachings and the new forms of voluntary religious association that they established provided their followers with new ways of thinking about themselves and their vocation in the world—a new narrative around which to construct their identities. As disembedded individuals, they understood the world as providing no permanent dwelling place. They were pilgrims, and they looked for their identity not in secure, established communities but in God's future in which they were called to participate. They were in many respects the first modern men and women—posttraditional individuals, restless seekers—and they helped to set in motion many of the changes that accelerated the pace of detraditionalization that we experience today.

In a provocative essay on postmodern life, sociologist Zygmunt Bauman (1995: 72–104) contrasts these early pilgrims with several new social types that he sees emerging as a result of the detraditionalizing processes that the reformers and others helped to set in motion. For the pilgrims, Calvinism provided a new narrative for their disembedded lives: a road to travel, a project or purpose in life toward which they moved through the world as sojourners. Postmodern (or posttraditional) life, however, is inhospitable to pilgrims. *"The hub of postmodern life is not identity building, but the avoidance of being fixed"* (Bauman 1995: 89). Thus, in contrast to pilgrims, the social types that characterize a postmodern world have no coherent story in which to locate themselves or their life course. Instead, they live their lives in fragments. Bauman describes four postmodern social types: "strollers," whose lives are a series of aimless episodes, without a past and without consequences; "vagabonds," who have no settled place but piece their trajectory together bit by bit; "tourists," who, unlike vagabonds, have homes, but nonetheless travel from place to place in search of adventure and excitement without ever becoming part of the places they visit; and, finally, "players," for whom life is a succession of self-enclosed games, each with its own rules. One plays each game wholeheartedly but works to insure that no game has any lasting consequences. It takes but little imagination to identify various acquaintances who exemplify Bauman's social types.

Not long ago these four lifestyles were found primarily among a minority of marginal individuals. Today, says Bauman, they characterize the majority. Time is no longer experienced as a river that flows from here to there. It is instead "a collection of ponds and pools." Strolling in particular conveys this episodic sense. Unlike the pilgrim who traveled with seriousness toward a goal, strolling is essentially aimless, without purpose. The stroller savors the scenery and his or her fleeting and inconsequential encounters with other strollers along the way. Bauman notes that it is not surprising that the modern shopping mall is an especially attractive social form. Malls, historically, were designed for strolling—for example, Washington's National Mall, the mall leading to Buckingham Palace (known simply as The Mall), and Pall Mall, London's fashionable shopping street. Today's malls are mostly for shopping. In them strollers can shop as they stroll and stroll as they shop in boutiques designed to meet their every need as well as to create new ones. Given the attraction of such malls, it is hardly surprising that new-style churches, with their plethora of small groups, not only resemble malls but are often referred to as "mall" churches.

What are some of the disembedding processes that are altering our relationship to traditions and fragmenting our lives? Consider what has happened to families, a key institution of memory. Changes include the shift away from growing up as part of extended families to being part of smaller nuclear families, often geographically removed from one's extended kin; the entry of women into the workforce in large numbers; changing perceptions of gender and parenting roles; and especially the dramatic rise in the divorce rate. In a 1997 survey, approximately 47 percent of those ages eighteen to thirty-four—Generation Xers as they are often called—reported that they had lived in a household where there was divorce, separation, or a single parent by the time they were eighteen. This was true for only 27 percent of those over age fifty-one.[16] Such changes take their toll on the family's capacity to bear traditions. They also foster a lack of trust in all traditional or tradition-bearing institutions—a characteristic trait of many members of Generation X.

Related to family change, geographic mobility is another important disembedding experience that removes us from stable, traditional communities and brings us regularly into contact with other communities, other traditions, and other ways of doing things. When our work moves us from one place to another across the continent and increasingly around the globe, or when we travel in other lands, we see new possibilities and are less constrained by the traditions and customs of any one community.

Let me illustrate what I mean with a simple, if now somewhat embarrassing, personal experience. In the late 1950s my wife and I spent a year in Scotland, where I was an assistant minister in a Church of Scotland parish. We had traveled to London and were having dinner in a restaurant. Boldly for us at that time, we decided to have wine with our meal. When the wine was served, I immediately began to worry: what if someone who knows me from back home in the United States comes into this London restaurant and sees me, a Methodist minister, drinking a glass of wine? I would not now want to try to calculate the odds of such an encounter happening; yet the authority of my Methodist teetotaler tradition still held enormous power over me. At the same time, however, I was experiencing the kind of individual freedom and choice open to me as I was disconnected from the communities and traditions that had shaped me in the past. In retrospect, this seems a trivial, if mildly amusing, story about my naivete—which I certainly exhibited. Yet multiply my experience by the enormous rate of mobility that we experience today, and try to calculate the considerable detraditionalizing impact that such mobility has. It is little wonder that *choice*—what Wade Clark Roof and William McKinney (1987) called the "new voluntarism"—is a dominant characteristic of posttraditional life, including religious participation. Authority is not "out there" in the tradition, but "in here" in our experience as disembedded, mobile selves who must therefore become authors of our own identities.

But it is not only geographic mobility that weakens the power of tradition and increases awareness of choice. Print and, especially, electronic media also connect us globally and contribute to our disembedding. Through television we experience distant events as they happen. Telephones, e-mail, and the Internet give us the means for instant communication with others far removed. Money and goods flow across national boundaries under the control of multinational corporations and multinational financial institutions. Expert knowledge is transferable from place to place. Ecological issues such as acid rain and depletion of the ozone layer or disasters such as Chernobyl are regular reminders of our global interdependence and citizenship. All of these factors indicate that local activities are no longer merely local, that the narratives by which we live and find meaning must take these global realities into account or lose their power to sustain us. In a documentary film on Islamic fundamentalism (York 1992), a group of Egyptian children who were students in a strict Muslim school were pictured on a school field trip during which the Qur'an was being read to them over the sound system of the bus. The narrator commented that the sound system was manufactured in Japan, the bus was made in Germany, and the roads on which they were traveling were paved with American foreign aid. At one stop on the tour, a Kentucky Fried Chicken restaurant was visible in the background. Maintaining the authority of tradition is not just a Western problem but an increasingly difficult prospect for all cultures in this global village. The old saying that followed the return of soldiers from World War I states the problem quite well: "When they've seen Paris, how can you keep them down on the farm?"—religiously as well as culturally.

Another crucial disembedding process, one that I have already alluded to in a variety of ways but that needs to be named explicitly, is cultural pluralism. One does not need to travel to another country or depend on the media to experience cultural or religious pluralism. Let me again be autobiographical. I grew up in a South Carolina town of approximately seven thousand people. Three Jewish families lived there along with a handful of Catholics. The rest of us were white and black Protestants representing no more than a dozen or so denominations. Even among Protestants, patterns of racial and economic segregation functioned to keep us from many serious encounters with each other's cultures. If there were gays and lesbians—and I am certain that there were—they were securely in the closet. Even the atheists and agnostics were fairly unrecognizable.

The contrast with my present community of residence is striking. In the subdivision of the midsized North Carolina city in which my wife and I live, within a half-mile radius of our home I can identify not only an assortment of evangelical and mainline Protestants of all races, but many Catholics and Jews as well as several Muslim families, Japanese Buddhists, an African family, a Hindu couple from India, and both gay and lesbian couples—and this represents the religious, ethnic, and cultural diversity only of those whom I encounter—admittedly not always in any deep way—on walks around the neighborhood. The local Yellow Pages lists fifty-plus different types of religious groups encompassing approximately four hundred congregations: churches, mosques, synagogues, and temples. This religious and cultural diversity is by no means atypical. If anything it considerably understates the diversity that one finds in some parts of the United States, especially California.

Religious and cultural diversity is, on balance, a positive experience; however, it takes its toll on traditional identities. As Peter Berger (1992: 68) has written, "Cultural plurality is experienced by the individual, not just as something external—all those people he bumps into—but as an internal reality, a set of options present in his mind. In other words, the different cultures he encounters in his social environment are transformed into alternative scenarios, options, for his own life." Thus, while the experience of such diversity can be both enriching and liberating, at the same time it often undercuts the capacity for certitude. It also fuels much of the anti-immigrant nativism that is on the rise in the United States and in other parts of the world. In short, it disembeds us at the level of consciousness.

Recalling these various disembedding processes is crucial for understanding the increasing loss of the authority of traditions that, as I noted previously, have been carried by institutions of memory. The changing nature of families and communities, travel, instantaneous communications, and encounters with diversity—these experiences make it increasingly difficult, especially for the young, to find their place in stable narratives or traditions both as sources of meaning for the present and as orientations for organizing one's future.

To be sure, not everyone experiences either the disembedding of social relationships or the questioning of one's taken-for-granted cultural perspectives to the same extent or in the same way. Even in our considerably detraditionalized society, many still live most of their lives in the same local contexts, in sharp contrast to highly mobile individuals who regularly encounter diverse cultures and traditions. Martin Marty (Carroll, Johnson, and Marty 1979: 89) once compared the situation to a large building that has two kinds of occupants: those who seldom leave their rooms, do the same tasks daily, and rarely encounter those who live in the other rooms (those whose orientation is primarily *local*); and those who roam the hallways, keenly aware of the diversity that exists, and who rarely meet anyone for whom traditional loyalties are important (those whose orientation is primarily *cosmopolitan*).

Sociologist Nancy Eiesland (Eiesland and Warner 1998: 52–54) introduces us to flesh-and-blood local and cosmopolitan types in her description of two families, the Englands and the Penners, whom she encountered in the course of a study of Dacula, Georgia, a former rural community caught up in exurban Atlanta. The Englands, now retired, have lived all of their lives and reared their family in Dacula, and the town encompasses most of their life—social, civic, economic, political, leisure, and religious. Most of their family also lives nearby. The Englands shop locally. They regularly meet a group of longtime friends for Saturday night dinner at a local restaurant. They join these friends on Sunday mornings at the local United Methodist church. Their Methodist identity is sufficiently strong that they outlasted a charismatic conflict that disrupted their congregation and led some other members to leave.

In contrast, the Penners are much more cosmopolitan in their orientation. Originally from other parts of the country, they moved to Dacula because of the attraction of the town's relatively low housing costs and its ease of access to a regional shopping center and other amenities of the metropolitan area. Access to interstate highways and the airport were also important, especially for Mr. Penner's work. Although the Penners have lived in Dacula for several years, they have established few local ties. Their friends and family are widely scattered. They shop in the regional malls and participate in cultural and leisure activities in the metropolitan area. Although they attend the same local United Methodist church as the Englands, they have relationships to other religious groups. For example, Mrs. Penner participates in a grief relief group in a local Baptist megachurch as she tries to come to grips with her mother's death, and they send their preschool child to a day-care program in a nearby Pentecostal congregation. In short, their day-to-day lives are much more disembedded and segmented than is true for the Englands. The Englands are locals, "room dwellers"; the Penners are cosmopolitans who "roam the hallways."

Differences in perspective between locals and cosmopolitans are a major contributor to the tensions and conflicts that we experience in congregational life and in the broader culture. Locals are much more likely to resist changes in traditional beliefs and practices in which they have found stable, meaningful identities. Cosmopolitans are more likely to question traditions, reinterpret them in light of their diverse and fragmented experiences, or simply reject them altogether. Many of the newer ecclesial forms that I consider in the following chapter represent efforts to minister to posttraditional cosmopolitans. Some—for example, the widespread popularity of small groups—are created for cosmopolitans as surrogates for the traditional institutions of memory that they no longer find helpful.

Despite the persistence of locals in a posttraditional world, those with cosmopolitan orientations—the strollers, the vagabonds, the tourists, and the players—are a growing majority in our society, and they are especially numerous among Baby Boomers and Generation Xers (also known as Baby Busters). The Boomers in particular are a generation of restless seekers (Roof 1993), and they are having a major impact on religion in and outside the churches. Theirs is a mobile, fluid quest for the sacred. It is tied less to institutions or places or traditional communities than to notions of journey or quest—more, however, like Bauman's strollers and tourists than like Bunyan's pilgrim. When Boomers have returned to churches and synagogues, they often look for strongly participatory congregations that encourage lay initiative and involvement, congregations that recognize their changed relationship to tradition and offer liturgy and music that connect with their cultural experiences. They value small groups that allow them to move in and out easily and in which they can find support and community and explore issues of faith. Some, frustrated by the overabundance of choices that a detraditionalized society presents, seek out congregations that offer clear, unambiguous teachings that limit choice. So we get a whole variety of types of innovations in local ecclesial practices: seeker churches, mall churches, cell churches, twelve-step groups, groups for meditation, Bible study groups, contemporary Christian music, and changes in architectural and liturgical styles, to name but a few. We also get responses such as the Pentecostal congregation that became Episcopalian, or the former evangelicals who have affiliated with the Orthodox communion. Both of these latter groups have sought to retraditionalize their lives, to reconnect with historic traditions, not because they have no choice in the matter but precisely because they do have a choice.[17] They *choose* to connect with a tradition that has not been their own because it connects them with a past that counters the rootlessness of posttraditional society.

Posttraditional society does not mean the end of tradition. It means instead a world in which traditions can be claimed, rejected, reinterpreted, or even invented, but not simply taken for granted and uncritically followed. Nor does it mean the end of religion. That has been the fallacy of some theories of secularization. If anything, questions of the meaning and purpose of life, for which religious traditions have historically offered authoritative answers, are raised anew, as for example in the spiritual searches of the Baby Boomers and Generation Xers. This, in turn, has a profound impact on ecclesiology—on how we structure our congregations and congregational practices. Will the old ways suffice? Will our traditional ways of "being church"—for example, our accustomed liturgies, eighteenth-century hymns, and traditional organizational forms—meet the religious needs of the newer generations? The newer ecclesial forms that are being invented in the present, with some success, suggest that the answer is no. As congregations have changed in the past to meet new social and cultural conditions, so today, we need new ecclesial patterns to meet the challenges of a posttraditional world.

Barth's words with which I began this chapter are thus an appropriate text for thinking about our traditional ecclesiologies: there is no intrinsically sacred sociology of the church, nor are there any intrinsically sacred traditions about how we are to order our own lives or our ecclesial forms and practices. There are, to be sure, traditions that we honor and value, including traditions about ways of ordering the life of the church. We ignore or treat these traditions lightly to our own impoverishment; yet, as valuable as they are, we must recognize them as human constructions. To paraphrase Jesus' words to the Pharisees: Traditions were made for people, not people for traditions, and this includes ecclesial traditions. The Reformers recognized this when they enunciated the principle, *ecclesia semper reformanda*. Therefore in the next chapter I turn to an analysis of some of the newer local ecclesiologies that are part of the current religious scene and that are efforts to give expression to the Reformers' principle in a detraditionalizing, if not yet wholly posttraditional, society.

2

Responding to Posttraditional Society: Resistance and/or Accommodation

No spires. No crosses. No robes. No clerical collars. No hard pews. No kneelers. No biblical gobbledygook. No prayerly rote. No fire, no brimstone. No pipe organs. No dreary eighteenth-century hymns. No forced solemnity. No Sunday finery. No collection plates. . . . Centuries of European tradition and Christian habit are deliberately being abandoned, clearing the way for the new, contemporary forms of worship and belonging.

Charles Trueheart (1996: 36)

In the preceding chapter, I introduced the term "detraditionalization"— to describe a major process affecting both culture and society that leads to describing our situation as posttraditional. Although detraditionalization was underway at least as early as the Reformation and the Enlightenment, and especially during the late nineteenth century, it has gained momentum in the latter half of this century. In a posttraditional world, traditions that we have taken for granted, familiar and habitual ways of doing things, are called into question. Authority shifts from "out there," whether it be in an inerrant scripture, an infallible teaching office, an authoritative confession of faith, or a prescribed polity, to "in here," to the self or the community. Posttraditional individuals or communities may choose to draw on older traditions for guidance, but they may also feel free to reinterpret or ignore them as circumstances dictate.

Or they may invent their own new traditions, often mixing different elements into something of a pastiche.

As I emphasized, American ecclesial forms have not been static, but have changed in response to broader changes taking place in the larger society and culture. Thus it should not be surprising to find efforts by church leaders to respond to the emerging posttraditional situation. In this chapter I want to look more closely at some of these responses. I do so by describing in some detail characteristics of the newer local ecclesiologies, especially that group of churches variously called "seeker," "mall," or "cell" churches. I refer to them collectively as posttraditional or new-style churches.

Some observers of contemporary church life, such as Lyle Schaller (e.g., 1992, 1993, 1996), are cheerleaders for bold ecclesial experimentation in the face of the social and cultural changes that we are facing in posttraditional society. Schaller argues especially that the future of the church lies with emulating the large posttraditional congregations—megachurches such as Willow Creek—which he refers to as "seven-day-a-week" churches. He believes that such congregations have much to teach traditional churches about how to reach out and minister to new and especially younger constituencies. I agree with Schaller that we can learn from these newer ecclesial forms, although I believe that he is much too uncritical in his embrace of them. In sharp contrast, others argue against efforts by churches to adapt to the kind of culture that I have described. My Duke University colleagues Stanley Hauerwas and William Willimon (1989, 1996) are examples. The church's task, they argue, is not to worry about relating to the culture but to be the church—"a living, breathing, viable community of faith" (1989: 47)—engaging in traditional Christian practices. The church must stand against the culture in faithfulness to God, yet without withdrawing from it in sectarian isolation. Although there is much to commend in this perspective, I cannot agree with their sweeping dismissal of ecclesial efforts to adapt to a posttraditional world. I argue instead that traditional churches can learn from these efforts through critical reflection on these newer ecclesial forms and adaptation of some of their practices.

Culture as a "Tool Kit"

To put these newer ecclesial forms and practices in perspective, I turn to a helpful perspective on culture and cultural change proposed by the sociologist Ann Swidler (1986). Swidler (p. 273) describes culture "as a 'tool kit' of symbols, stories, rituals, and world-views, which people may use in varying configurations to solve different kinds of problems." They do so by creating "'strategies of action,' persistent ways of ordering [life and] action through time." We can think of ecclesial forms and practices as examples of strategies of action that church leaders have constructed under varying circumstances to solve problems they confront. Some are old, tried and true. Others are new and often controversial. Such strategies include organizational forms, leadership patterns, symbols, ritual practices, music, decision-making styles, and various types of programs. All of these are part of the cultural tool kits of denominations, congregations, and their leaders, developed at one time or another to address practical issues.

Swidler contrasts the role that culture plays in what she calls "settled periods" with its role in "unsettled periods." In settled times, culture provides materials from which people construct broad, well-established strategies of action that become traditions that anchor and integrate their lives. The strategies or traditions are like well-worn paths that one travels to get from here to there. One does not have to stop and think about them. Even when people do not always act in the ways that their traditions dictate, their lack of consistency does not call the traditions into question. They continue to be taken for granted as right and inevitable. They are accepted as authoritative even when they are not fully followed.

In contrast, in unsettled times, older cultural patterns are found wanting and are jettisoned. Entrepreneurial leaders draw from the cultural tool kit to develop and create new meaning systems, new cultural styles, new strategies of action to meet the challenges of unsettled times. As examples of "cultural entrepreneurs," Swidler cites the Reformers, especially John Calvin. Furthermore, in unsettled times, innovations in ritual practice or doctrine become highly charged emotionally, because "ritual changes reorganize taken-for-granted habits and modes of experience" (p. 279). They sometimes require a break with established, embedded, traditional ways of life; thus it is not surprising that conflicts, often severe in intensity, arise between those who promote new cultural models and practices and those who are reluctant to abandon familiar strategies of action.

Swidler's distinction between settled and unsettled periods is quite helpful in understanding the global shift as we increasingly experience detraditionalizing processes that disembed us from stable communities and familiar practices. Such experiences are unsettling, especially when well-worn paths of tradition no longer seem able to get us to our hoped-for destination. Instead, we confront choices unimaginable even a half century ago. Swidler's distinction is also extremely useful as a perspective for considering what is happening to churches, and to religion more generally. As I indicated previously, the move away from tradition is not absolute. It is more a "both-and" rather than an "either-or" matter. Nonetheless, detraditionalization unsettles things, and we are certainly more in an unsettled, posttraditional world today than in a traditional or settled one.

Thus I suggest that we can think of the various newer local ecclesiologies—the several types of seeker or cell or "next" churches, new worship and music styles, the multiplicity of small groups, even emerging new denominational configurations, and the conflicts that swirl around these innovations—as elements of new strategies of action constructed as efforts to meet the challenges of unsettled, detraditionalized times. They are strategies of action—some new and some refurbished older strategies—that entrepreneurial leaders have developed in response to the challenges of ministry in posttraditional society. These leaders view older, more traditional congregational forms as no longer adequate to meet new challenges. Here is how one of them characterizes traditional church life: "Preaching is insipid and unrelated to daily life. Fellowship means little more than superficial conversations in the church lobby after a service. Communion is an autopilot ritual, and prayer a formality. Surprises—in terms of programs or sermons or policies or life transformations—seldom occur, and a sense of the miraculous is an outdated notion. The 'haves' give little thought and even less help to the 'have nots.' The church operates as an isolated island of subculture, wondering why it is ignored and unappreciated by the community at large" (Hybels and Hybels 1995: 49). Although this characterization borders on caricature, it reveals the passion with which new-style church leaders set themselves over against traditional practices. In turn, because their new strategies of action sharply challenge traditional, deeply revered ecclesial practices, they are sharply criticized and often dismissed by those of us who are comfortable with and accustomed to the older ways.

Responses to Unsettled Times

In what follows, I describe several of these newer local ecclesiological responses, using Swidler's perspective to understand them as responses to the unsettling that detraditionalization brings to traditional ways of doing things. In doing so, I draw on my own and others' research. Even so, I have to be highly selective. There is simply no way to capture the variety that exists. Although my primary interest is in posttraditional or new-style churches, it is instructive to locate them on a continuum of ecclesial and quasi-ecclesial responses to detraditionalization. At one end are various forms of resistance to detraditionalizing processes; at the opposite end are those reflecting a high degree of accommodation. Post-traditional congregations, which fall along the continuum, reflect elements of each. I do not discuss more conventional, mainstream congregations, not only because most readers are quite familiar with their ecclesial practices, but also because we often learn from paying attention to what may be called the outliers, those that push the envelope in one direction or another. I am particularly interested in adaptive responses that might be called reflexive or reflective. They are responses that neither resist detraditionalization nor simply accommodate to it. Rather they self-consciously redefine situations, drawing on and reinterpreting traditional beliefs and patterns in light of new experiences.

Resistance

At the resistance pole, the most visible forms of intentional opposition to detraditionalization are the various expressions of global fundamentalism, including fundamentalist Protestant congregations, that have made active opposition to detraditionalizing forces a central thrust of their ecclesial and theological distinctiveness. They are committed to asserting the truth of their tradition with little regard for the consequences. For Christian fundamentalists, that truth is found in an inerrant scripture, and their resistance is both institutional and ideological.

It is a mistake to consider fundamentalists as premodern, nor are they attempting to turn back the clock to a premodern time. Rather, it is more accurate to view them as creations of modernity. They would not exist without modernity, and they use many of its fruits, especially technology, for their own purposes. They are, however, profoundly *anti*modern, opposing the ideology and ethics of modernism (and of posttraditional society), particularly the emphasis on individual autonomy, choice, and tolerance of diversity. Sociologist Nancy Ammerman (1987: 8–9) makes this point when she argues that fundamentalists are not found primarily in the backwaters of society, where traditional beliefs and practices are still alive, well, and widely respected. Rather they are most likely found where traditions encounter modernity and detraditionalizing forces—in middle-class suburbs, for example. There people who grew up in rural communities and small towns encounter an agnostic urban world and find it untenable. Those whom Ammerman studied, members of Southside Gospel Church, a fundamentalist congregation in a suburb of a New England industrial city, were solidly middle class in occupations, education, and income. A similar profile is characteristic of members of

Jerry Falwell's well-known Thomas Road Baptist Church in Lynch-burg, Virginia.

Although fundamentalist believers can be found in many congregations, including liberal ones, it is in fundamentalist congregations that ecclesiology becomes a primary strategy of action for resisting detraditionalization. At Southside Gospel Church, Thomas Road Church, and in literally thousands of other large and small fundamentalist congregations like them, the aim is to separate believers as much as possible from detraditionalizing influences. They aim at becoming all-encompassing institutions, creating alternative social and cultural worlds that encapsulate as much as possible of their members lives—much like the pre-Vatican II Catholic Church in the late nineteenth and early twentieth centuries. Here is how Frances Fitzgerald (1986: 138) describes Falwell's Thomas Road Church:

> The Thomas Road Church is a great deal more than a house for prayers. It is a vast and mighty institution, with some sixty pastors and about a thousand volunteer helpers and trainees. It has Lynchburg Christian Academy, the summer camp, and Liberty Baptist College, whose students worship and work in the church. In addition, it has separate ministries for children, young people, adults, elderly people, the deaf, the retarded, and the imprisoned. Last year, it added a ministry for divorced people and another one for unmarried young adults. On Sundays, the church holds three general services and has Sunday-school classes for children of every age group, from the nursery on up. But it is a center of activity every day of the week. There is a general prayer meeting every Wednesday night. Then, every week each ministry offers a program of activities for its age group, including Bible-study classes, lectures, trips, sports outings, and picnics. The ministries also organize groups of volunteers to visit hospitals, nursing homes, and prisons and to proselytize in the community. The organization is so comprehensive that any Thomas Road member, old or young, could spend all his or her time in church or in church-related activities. In fact, many church members do just that.

In such an alternative world, members are shielded from the disembedding, detraditionalizing forces that accompany modernity. Not only Christian schools but the increasingly popular home schooling movement (no longer exclusively a conservative Christian practice) are further examples of a resistance strategy, as are also Christian radio and television stations and businesses run by born-again Christians that are listed

in Christian Yellow Pages. Family life and friendships are also encapsu-
lated within the community of fellow believers and are key arenas for sus-
taining an alternative worldview.

Added to their institutional and social forms of resistance, fundamentalist congregations offer clear, authoritative (often authoritarian)
teaching that allows little room for individual autonomy, choice, or dis-
sent. Their teaching is based on the belief in the absolute authority of
the Bible, which is further buttressed by the conviction that the Bible is
totally without error. In a sensitively filmed television documentary
about another New England fundamentalist congregation (Ault and
Camerini 1987), one of the members described how he and his wife rely
on his pastor's help in resolving disputes: "The beautiful thing about
having a church where the pastor is a fundamentalist is we can call him
up and ask him where in God's Word to find the answer to our dilemma.
And we don't call him up to ask him his opinion—because he's a man
the same as I am with as many if not more problems than me. So, you
know, what I want to know is where in God's Word I can find the answer.
And because he's called of God, he turns around and he can tell me
where the passages are in the Bible that pertain to my problem. And let
the Holy Spirit answer." This is one way of resisting the shift of authority from "out there" to "in here" and for dealing with the plethora of
choices characteristic of posttraditional society.

Not all strong resisters are fundamentalists in the strict sense of the
word—that is, believers in certain "fundamentals" of the faith, especially
an inerrant scripture and separation from the world. Some of the fundamentalists' forms of resistance are also used by other conservative or
evangelical Protestant groups: Pentecostals, for example, and congregations affiliated with conservative Reformed denominations, such as the
Orthodox Presbyterian Church and the Presbyterian Church in America.
Both Pentecostals and conservative Reformed churches believe in the
absolute authority of the Bible, the physical resurrection of Jesus, the
necessity of a born-again experience, and other orthodox Christian
beliefs that also characterize fundamentalism. Although they do not
always hold to the strict separatism characteristic of hard-core fundamentalists, they also often construct alternative institutions, especially
Christian schools, and they emphasize traditional gender roles and family patterns. The Reformed groups also place considerable stock in the
church's tradition, especially the Reformed tradition, unlike most fundamentalists, who skip over centuries of church tradition to get "back to
the Bible." In interviews with young adults who have joined conservative Reformed congregations, Richard Cimino (1997) found that they

have done so as a way of escaping and challenging the individualism, fragmentation, and pluralism of posttraditional society. He discovered, however, that, characteristic of posttraditional society, those he interviewed did not accept the whole of the Reformed tradition. They picked and chose, emphasizing some parts, ignoring others. As he says, they "have retrieved and reformulated elements . . . which best provide authoritative 'answers' to the overriding realities of society they have faced as young adults" (p. 62), especially pluralism, fragmentation, and the erosion of traditional sources of moral authority and meaning.[1]

Similarly, recall my reference in the introduction to the Assemblies of God congregation in Georgia that chose, as a congregation, to join the Episcopal Church out of a desire to connect to historic Christian traditions—though without losing much of the spontaneity of their Pentecostal heritage. I also cited the group of nineteen evangelicals, leaders of Campus Crusade for Christ, who left the organization and evangelicalism in the early 1980s to join the Orthodox communion. They have founded a number of growing congregations across the United States affiliated with the Antiochian Orthodox Archdiocese. This dramatic shift was for them and others who have followed them into Orthodoxy an effort to resist accommodation to modernity. Such accommodation, they perceived, was taking place in evangelical as well as mainline Protestantism and was eroding the timeless truth of the gospel. Not only does Orthodoxy, with its claim to be the one true New Testament church, provide them with a true lineage to the apostles, but it also resists change. One evangelical who made the shift said in a radio interview that liking or not liking is foreign to Orthodoxy. If evangelicals do not like a particular congregation's beliefs or practices, they leave and go to another that they do like. In contrast, Orthodoxy says, "This is the faith. You don't like it or not like it" (Burnett 1997).

The appeal of these various efforts to resist detraditionalization is strong, and it is not limited to Christians. For example, sociologist Lynn Davidman (1991) studied two groups of Jewish women who have returned to Orthodox Judaism as a way of resisting the confusion over gender roles and family patterns and the lack of an ordered sense of self and community that they experienced in the wider society. One group turned to an Orthodox synagogue, the other to a Hasidic intentional community. In both instances, the women were reconnected to an established religious tradition that gave them "a sense of being rooted in some firm, stable and clearly defined way of being" (Davidman 1991: 93). It also gave them an unambiguous sense of their identity as women by prescribing clear role definitions for men and women. The Hasidic community, like some fundamentalist Christian communities, created an alternative social world where the women lived together with minimal outside contacts, wore distinctive dress, and were regularly involved in teaching by the community's rabbis. The synagogue was less able to create an actual alternative social world for its participants, but sought to do so by a variety of shared practices and also by what Davidman calls a creative reinterpretation of the tradition—an example of reflexivity, as I am using that term here.

To summarize: These resisters—both strong and mild—to detraditionalization do so by creating, as much as is possible, an institutional and ideological religious subculture that provides an alternative to dominant features of posttraditional society. They stand in sharp contrast to those on the opposite end of the continuum.

Accommodation

At this opposite pole are individuals and groups (one can hardly call some of them congregations) that have accommodated to posttraditional society. In sharp contrast to fundamentalists and other resisters who have strongly opposed detraditionalizing processes by their ecclesial forms and practices, accommodationists have adapted their religious styles to it.

The epitome of accommodation, hardly warranting being called an ecclesial response, is the example of a young nurse, Sheila Larson, profiled by Robert Bellah and his colleagues in *Habits of the Heart* (1985: 220–21). In describing her faith, she says, "I believe in God. I'm not a religious fanatic. I can't remember the last time I went to church. My faith has carried me a long way. It's Sheilaism. Just my own little voice." Bellah and his colleagues comment that at one time, Anne Hutchinson, a seventeenth-century precursor of Sheila, was run out of the Massachusetts Bay Colony for following her own inner voice. Today this kind of response is becoming the norm, as people who live with no connection to a tradition or narrative become "sects unto themselves," to use Thomas Jefferson's description. In telephone interviews with 1,150 residents of North Carolina and southern California, Wade Clark Roof and I found that 66 percent agreed that a person should arrive at his or her religious beliefs independently of any church or religious group. Seventy-three percent of those ages 18 to 34 were in agreement. Although many of these people are members of congregations, their responses mirror a mild form of "Sheilaism."[2]

Another fairly widespread type of accommodation, a kind of restless spiritual seeking that is not unlike Sheilaism in its individualism, is typified in a young Jewish woman described by the theologian Arthur Green (1994). Green discovered her through her self-description in a newspaper personals column: *"DJF, 34. Spiritual, not religious. Seeking like-minded JM, etc."* Treating her as an "icon of our age," Green characterizes her further: She can sometimes be found at weekend Kripalu Yoga Ashram retreats, "where she goes for Yoga, massage, a lecture on spiritual teachings, healthy vegetarian food, and conversations with like-minded people." She fasts and meditates on Yom Kippur, celebrates "totally unspiritual" Passovers with her family, and reads both Hasidic and Sufi stories. "She thinks of herself as a seeker rather than a joiner," and this is the meaning of her distinction between being spiritual rather than religious. "She picks things up here and there, believes that all religions are one, and is happy to live with bits of turned-on teachings from Jewish, Sufi, Hindu, and Buddhist sources all joined without any need for theological consistency." By "spiritual, not religious," she also signals that she is not interested in a relationship with an Orthodox Jewish guy or the traditional Jewish lifestyle that a relationship with him would require. Such a lifestyle, she believes, would "'lay a trip on her' about observance and exclude her as a woman."

Although it is obvious that this young woman's response to posttraditional society is strikingly different from that of the previously noted Jewish women who joined the Orthodox congregations, she is in many ways their "soul sister." Like them she seeks for a way of dealing with the rootlessness and anomie that come from being thrown back on one's own self as the authority in one's life. Unlike them, however, she looks not to Orthodoxy but tries to find wisdom in whatever traditions or narratives seem to offer guidance. As was true for Sheilaism, her seeking can be called an "ecclesial" response primarily in the Jeffersonian sense of being a sect to one's self.

Less blatantly individualistic than either this young woman or Sheila Larson but still standing near the accommodative end of the continuum are many of the small groups that currently flourish, some with church sponsorship, others, such as house churches, institutionally independent. Liliane Voyé (1995), a sociologist in Belgium, studied a number of small groups of the latter type. Participants are mostly disaffected Catholics who claim Christian inspiration not through the institutional church but through the Bible, the life of Christ, and the witness of communities such as Taizé. Yet she found that participants retain only selected elements from the Christian tradition. These they choose and interpret themselves, and, like the young Jewish woman, they often combine them with ingredients borrowed from other religions in bricolage or pastiche fashion—the kind of mixing of codes that is characteristic of a posttraditional world. It was common, she reports, to hear statements such as: "You must be able to make your way by yourself; you must not be obliged to pray, or attend the Eucharist, or have to affirm certain things, or teach certain things." Such groups are generally led by lay people; if a priest is present, he is simply a member of the group, of equal status with the others.

Similar Catholic (and Protestant) groups are found in this country as well.[3] In Robert Wuthnow's (1994) research on small groups in the United States, he found that a majority of these small groups, in which approximately 40 percent of the population participate, are religious or spiritual in character, offering opportunities for spiritual growth, support, and a caring community. Many are church-sponsored; others, like those in Belgium, are relatively autonomous. Although Wuthnow found much that is positive about these small groups, some of their characteristics clearly reflect the impact of detraditionalization. For example, many place a high premium on respect for diversity. In doing so they encourage members to regard all points of view as equally valid rather than engaging in the hard work of finding a common ground in, for example, the meaning of a biblical text. Members often create their own versions of spirituality, as in the Belgian groups. They mix elements from different religious traditions. One result is that each member, as Wuthnow says, "walks away with an individualized, distinctive version—largely because spirituality remains personal and subjective." Furthermore, "Small groups encourage many members to regard biblical wisdom as truth only if it somehow helps them to get along better in their daily lives. Groups generate a do-it-yourself religion, a God who makes life easier, a programmed form of spirituality that robs the sacred of its awe-inspiring mystery and depth. . . . In simplest terms, the sacred comes to be associated with small insights that seem intuitively correct to the small group rather than wisdom accrued over the centuries in hermitages, seminaries, universities, congregations, and church councils" (1994: 357–58). Wuthnow also notes how privately and inwardly focused the spirituality expressed in many small groups is—a reflection of the shift of authority from "out there" in a tradition or an institution to the subjective experience of the individual or, in this case, the small group.

One may object that these forms that I have cited hardly deserve to be considered as ecclesiologies. Yet for many people, such groups are their congregation, where they turn for meaning, support, and guidance in their fragmented lives. Although they may not jettison the Bible or some practices from the church's tradition, they often mix insights from them with elements from other traditions as components of the tool kit that they use to construct their religious identity. Such efforts reflect—some more and some less—what Ernst Troeltsch (1912: 381–82) called mysticism, a third social form of Christianity along with the church and the sect. In one sense, mysticism implies a profound religious experience that is the experiential basis for both churches and sects. But mysticism had a broader meaning for Troeltsch. It signifies a personal, subjective form of religion, an independent attitude. It is more individual than institutional, more immediate and experiential than rooted in church tradition or scripture. It permits widely differing views of the central truths of the religion.[4] If fundamentalism reflects the sectarian response, then much that transpires in individual spirituality and the spirituality of small groups leans toward Troeltschian mysticism. Troeltsch believed that mysticism was on the rise as the "secret religion" of the educated classes. The problem with mysticism, as he was keenly aware, is its lack of an institutional base and of communal myths, symbols, rituals, and other ecclesial practices that sustain religious faith over time and in the face of adversity or challenge. It is a "journey" or movable spirituality rather than one tied to a particular place and community. Because they lack an institutional base, many of the mystical or accommodative expressions of religion that I described are likely to be short-lived and ephemeral, but perhaps they are well suited to the seekers who stroll in the religious shopping malls of posttraditional society.

Accommodation and *Resistance: Posttraditional Congregations*

Most local ecclesial responses to detraditionalization, including those of more conventional, mainstream churches, fall somewhere between the two poles of hard-line resistance and extreme accommodation. They adapt to detraditionalizing influences by combining elements of resistance with accommodation. This is especially true of those congregations that I am calling posttraditional or new style, which are my principal concern in this chapter. Such congregations are also variously known as megachurches, mall churches, cell churches, or what an article in a popular journal called "next" churches (Trueheart 1996). In his important study of three examples of such churches (congregations affiliated with the Calvary Chapel, Hope Chapel, and Vineyard Christian Fellowship movements), sociologist Donald Miller (1997) refers to them as "new paradigm" or "postmodern" churches.[5] These several labels are used to describe churches that are self-conscious reactions to posttraditional society even if they do not name it as such. Their leaders have made a deliberate, reflexive effort, however controversial, to respond to some of its characteristics and to adapt their ecclesial practices to the new situation. Although these churches are not clones of one another, they share many similarities. They do so in large part because of the early successes of pioneer congregations such as Willow Creek Community Church in Great Barrington, Illinois. To paraphrase the television commercial for the brokerage firm E. F. Hutton, when Willow Creek speaks—that is, when its leaders develop new strategies of action that seem to succeed in responding to a cultural crisis such as the hemorrhaging of members from traditional churches—others listen and emulate.

In no way do I claim intimate knowledge of the broad variety of these nontraditional congregations. Also, as I have indicated previously, I am not an apologist for them. There is much that troubles me about them. At the same time I find a great deal that is intriguing and challenging. Learning from them may help us in the task of rebuilding the ecosystems of faith that are needed if we are to revitalize mainstream Protestant churches. Because much has been written about these churches in the popular press, many readers are familiar with their dominant characteristics. Nonetheless, I will highlight several of their more striking attributes that can be interpreted as strategic responses to the unsettling character of a posttraditional world. In doing so, I draw on insights from visits to a number of these congregations[6] as well as published and unpublished studies of these new-style churches. What then are some of the primary characteristics of these congregations, and how do they represent new, posttraditional strategies of action?

One characteristic, so well known that it seems hardly worth mentioning, is that most of these congregations are large. Some of them are *very* large. For example, Willow Creek has approximately fifteen thousand members. Thus they are called "megachurches," which has come to refer to congregations with twenty-five hundred or more members. The number of these congregations has been growing, especially congregations not affiliated with a denomination, but also within denominations, including mainline traditions. They stand in sharp relief next to the vast majority of all Protestant congregations. In most Protestant denominations, especially mainline Protestant, between 50 and 60 percent of all congregations have two hundred or fewer members. For example, 60 percent of United Methodist congregations average seventy-five or fewer in attendance, and 32 percent average thirty-five or less.

Their large size gives the new-style congregations material and human resources to develop high quality, professionally presented programs. It also gives people who join them a sense of being part of something big and important, and it makes it possible for a congregation to provide multiple programs that address needs and concerns of a variety of people. Such programs provide many entry points for newcomers. Because, as we shall see, the multiple programs are typically organized in terms of small groups, new-style congregations are able to balance the benefits of largeness with the warmth, intimacy, mutual support, and accountability that, at their best, small groups provide.

I noted earlier that these congregations share characteristics of both ends of the resistance-accommodation continuum. Thus, reflecting the resistance pole, most are on the conservative or evangelical side of the theological and ecclesiastical spectrum, even if they are affiliated with a more liberal or mainstream denomination.[7] Despite sharing some characteristics of fundamentalism, including emphasis on the sole authority of the scriptures, they are not separatist or sectarian. Instead, much of their ecclesial style represents a pragmatic effort to adapt if not accommodate to life in a posttraditional world. Indeed, as Miller (1997: 127–28) points out, many of them do not place a high premium on purity of theological doctrine. "There are a lot of people who have their theology down but are not in love with Jesus," he quotes one Calvary Chapel pastor as saying. Beliefs are important, but a right personal relationship with Jesus takes precedence. Similarly, I have heard several pastors of posttraditional churches use the expression: "We major in the majors, and minor in the minors." That is, certain beliefs are major: the sole authority of scripture, the divinity and physical resurrection of Christ, justification by faith, and the Trinity. Less important doctrines and lifestyle issues are considered minors and permit differences of interpretation.

Also, like fundamentalists, these posttraditional congregations view themselves as true heirs of New Testament congregations who have been able to dispose of the outdated, accumulated baggage of tradition. They claim to "leapfrog" centuries of tradition to get back to how they assumed the primitive church functioned. They find biblical precedent for their innovations, drawing especially from the second chapter of Acts as the primary source for a model of a Spirit-led church. This "primitivist impulse," as historian Grant Wacker (1995: 142) describes it with reference to Pentecostalism, represents "a powerfully destructive urge to smash all humanmade traditions in order to return to a first-century world where the Holy Spirit alone reigned." Alexander Campbell, looked to as the founder both of the relatively liberal Christian Church (Disciples of Christ) and the conservative Churches of Christ, endorsed primitivism as a return to the "ancient order of things."

As the reference to Campbell illustrates, the primitivist impulse is not new. Evangelical congregations have almost always sat more lightly to inherited traditions than mainline churches, but the belief that they are patterning their congregations after the New Testament church gives posttraditional congregations license to innovate or at least to ignore traditional ecclesial practices. This is an important difference between them and mainstream Protestants. While most mainstream Protestants, like evangelicals, subscribe to *sola scriptura*, they are often more constrained than many evangelicals by respect for their historic traditions and polities. Traditions and polity tend to put the brakes on innovations that appear immoderate. Instead, they foster a concern to do things "decently and in order," as Presbyterians sometimes put it. In the next chapter, I return to the importance of traditions for establishing boundaries that are crossed with great caution.

Because of their conservative theological stance, combined with primitivist impulses and a concern for cultural relevance, Donald Miller (1997: 25) refers to the Vineyard, Calvary Chapel, and Grace Chapel congregations as "postmodern primitivists." As he says, these churches "acknowledge and utilize many aspects of postmodern culture, yet they find in the biblical tradition—especially the 'primitive Christianity' of the first century—an underpinning for a radical spirituality that undermines the cynicism and fragmentation of many postmodern theorists." Moreover, many posttraditional congregations have been blessed with innovative, entrepreneurial leaders who have combined the primitivist impulse with a complementary pragmatism[8] in shaping their congregations' ecclesial strategies of action. They have demonstrated a capacity to see a need and find creative ways of meeting it. Often claiming the authority of the apostle Paul to "become all things to all people, that [they] might by all means save some" (2 Corinthians 9:22), they have been unwilling to be bound by the conventions of the Christian tradition.

When one thinks of innovative, entrepreneurial leaders, one thinks of Bill Hybels and his colleagues who developed Willow Creek Community Church. There are also the Californians: the late John Wimber, founder of the Vineyard Christian Fellowship; Chuck Smith, founder of Calvary Chapel; Ralph Moore, founder of the Hope Chapel movement; Rick Warren, founder of the Saddleback Valley Community Church; Dieter Zander, founder of New Song Community Church; and especially Robert Schuller, founding pastor of the Crystal Cathedral, who pioneered several of the strategies of action that others have emulated and carried farther. The use of the familiar form of their first name by several leaders—Bill, Chuck, and Rick, for example—suggests a conscious effort to be informal and folksy in a world where tradition smacks of formality. It also is an important way of minimizing the symbolic distance between clergy and laity that is an important characteristic of these churches.[9]

That several of these posttraditional congregations have their origins in California is probably not coincidental. California is arguably one of the most "unsettled" (in Swidler's sense), detraditionalized regions of the United States. Its unsettled character is no doubt a key factor in spawning the cultural innovations, including religious innovations, that occur there and then spread across the nation. A section of a recent book on resurgent evangelicalism (Shibley 1996) has the intriguing title, "The Californication of Conservative Protestantism." (Some critics of new-style churches will agree that both implications of Shibley's title are accurate.)

Although many of the primary leaders of posttraditional congregations are ordained pastors who have been trained in theological seminaries or Bible colleges, many of their staff members, some paid and others volunteer, have been "raised up" from within the congregation. They are lay members who are identified as having spiritual gifts and encouraged and trained to initiate ministries that will use their particular gifts, for example, with children or youth or as leaders of a small group, or as pastors of new satellite congregations. Indeed, much of the work of these churches is carried out by lay members—some paid, but many who are volunteers. The practice of providing their own training programs has led some of the larger congregations to form a network of teaching churches whose programs are attended by members sent to them from other congregations. Such programs, though not accredited, compete with seminary programs that have traditionally offered training in these specialized areas of work. Indeed, some pastors of these larger congregations have been highly critical of traditional seminary education, because they believe not only that much of it is irrelevant, but that it also creates too much distance between graduates and the laity in the congregations whom they serve. The emphasis in posttraditional congregations on lay ministries and other efforts to reduce the symbolic distance between clergy and laity reflect what Miller (1997: 80) calls a "democratization of access to the sacred."

Yet another characteristic of posttraditional congregations has been their high degree of intentionality in identifying both their purpose and their primary audience. To do so, they have drawn pragmatically and unashamedly on language and techniques from the corporate world. They use market research to identify their "target market" and to understand the characteristics and needs of those whom they have identified; they develop mission statements to clarify their direction; and they engage in strategic planning. It is, perhaps, no accident that Peter Drucker, a leading consultant to corporate America, has become a major guru to new-style pastors and cheerleader of their "pastoral" congregations, as he calls them. Although mixing business and religion is not new in religion generally and in American religion especially,[10] this deliberate use of corporate, market-oriented language in developing strategies of action for the church is a striking characteristic of these congregations. It is also an ecclesial example of the mixing of codes or bricolage quality typical of groups as well as individuals in posttraditional society.

In their mission or vision statements, most posttraditional congregations describe their primary task as bringing people to Christian maturity, which involves both evangelism and nurture. Creating "Fully Devoted Followers of Christ" is how several, Willow Creek included, express this two-pronged mission. In the Generation-X-oriented New Song Church in Covina, California, the phrase is not only central to their mission statement but also emblazoned on T-shirts inscribed with the letters FDFX, an acronym for "Fully Devoted Followers of Christ." The congregations aim not only at bringing new members into the church—the evangelistic task—but also at leading them to a deeper sense of Christian discipleship—"discipling" them is the term that is used—in ways that we shall consider below.

Whereas New Song's target audience is members of Generation X, Willow Creek's, at least initially,[11] was members of the Baby Boom generation, typified by the now well-known composite individual, "Unchurched Harry," who, they said, "is probably in his family room with his feet up on the footstool reading the paper or watching TV with a can of beer in his hand." Like their fellow Baby Boomers, "Unchurched Harry," and his female counterpart, "Unchurched Mary," have experienced considerable detraditionalization. How, Willow Creek's leaders asked, do we bring Unchurched Harry "out of his chair all the way to a point of Christian maturity?" "How do we lead Harry and Mary to become 'Fully Devoted Followers of Christ'?"

Willow Creek's market research suggested five reasons that such individuals were indifferent to the church: (1) churches were always asking for money, while often nothing significant seemed to be done with it; (2) church services were boring and lifeless; (3) church services were predictable; (3) sermons were irrelevant to daily life in the real world; and (4) the pastor made people feel guilty and ignorant, so they leave church feeling worse than when they entered. These assumptions about their target audience have been the basis for many of Willow Creek's innovative strategies, including their now much-copied and controversial seeker service. So impressive has been their marketing strategy that Harvard Business School has prepared a teaching case for study by business students (Mellado 1991). Using marketing to achieve their purpose, they have tried to give people what they want, while at the same time they also "give them what they didn't know they wanted—a life change," as one posttraditional church pastor expressed it (Trueheart 1996: 40).

Another striking yet common characteristic of many posttraditional churches—a consequence of their market research—is that their buildings do not typically look or feel like traditional churches, nor are their sanctuaries appointed with traditional Christian symbols.[12] In the passage cited above in the epigraph, Charles Trueheart begins an *Atlantic Monthly* (1996: 37) article describing these churches as follows: "No spires. No crosses. No robes. No clerical collars. No hard pews. No kneelers. No biblical gobbledygook. No prayerly rote. No fire, no brimstone. No pipe organs. No dreary eighteenth-century hymns. No forced solemnity. No Sunday finery. No collection plates." "This list," he continues, "has asterisks and exceptions, but its meaning is clear. Centuries of European tradition and Christian habit are deliberately being abandoned, clearing the way for the new, contemporary forms of worship and belonging."

For a visitor to Willow Creek, the long winding drive through the campus to the church's buildings gives the feeling that one is making a pilgrimage. Yet what the pilgrim finds when arriving at the shrine is not a space that marks off boundaries that separate the sacred from the profane, as traditional church architecture has often done. Nor does the pilgrim experience a sense of God's otherness and mystery that one might in a cathedral or temple. Instead, the buildings and campus could easily be mistaken for a corporate headquarters like those in which many of their Boomer congregation work. Although messages about the sacred are heard in the buildings, the buildings themselves emulate the profane. What is true at Willow Creek is also true of many posttraditional congregations, some of whom have paid even less attention to traditional church architecture.

Having outgrown their original facilities, Crossroads Fellowship in Raleigh, North Carolina, an eight-year-old, two-thousand-plus member congregation, purchased a former warehouse in an industrial park for their new church building. Other congregations meet in former movie theaters, or, as New Song Church does, in a public school gymnasium, where they have to set up and then break things down again for each service. Leaders at New Song say that there is something "New Testament-like" about having to re-create their worship space each week.[13]

When new-style churches do build their own facilities, as Willow Creek did, or purchase existing space, they seek to locate them near expressways and other major highways. They do not understand themselves to be neighborhood congregations or local churches serving a fixed community. They draw instead from a broad region. The churches themselves are disembedded, much like the constituencies they serve.

In the place of traditional symbols, stained glass, and other appointments that we have come to associate with a church through the centuries, one often finds movable, cushioned chairs—sometimes theater-style seats—rather than hard, fixed pews; low ceilings rather than vaulting naves; a low platform with a clear plexiglass podium rather than a pulpit. The plexiglass does not come between the preacher and the congregation in the way that a pulpit does. There are also the inevitable overhead projectors and screens for projecting hymns and praise choruses. A cartoon in *Christianity Today* (March 7, 1994) depicted an American pastor who was touring Notre Dame Cathedral in Paris. There is a fatal flaw, he thought: "No blank walls for projecting praise choruses!" At Chapel Hill Bible Church, Jim Abrahamson, whose title is teaching pastor, also effectively uses an overhead projector to outline the points of his sermons. Organs are also out. In their place are guitars, keyboards, synthesizers, and drums. In the case of the Generation-X-oriented New Song Church, whose Internet Web site describes it as a place "Where the Flock Likes to Rock," there is a seven piece rock band. In the Christian Faith Center, a large African-American congregation in North Carolina, a twenty piece band and several groups of singers lead the congregation in rollicking gospel music.

The music, especially, that has become one of the most notable and controversial features of posttraditional congregations. Although some continue to include traditional hymns, all include some forms of contemporary Christian music, especially praise choruses with simple, often biblically based lyrics that are repeated over and over[14]—for example:

> Yahweh, Yahweh
> Ancient One yet you're here today
> Ageless One, Changeless One
> Showing love to all generations
>
> Show us your glory, O Lord
> Let your glory pass before us
> Right before our eyes
>
> And we will worship, and we will bow down
> And we will call you Lord

And we will kneel before
The maker of the universe
And we will call you Lord

Yahweh, Yahweh
Faithful One, you have shown us the way
Through the years, through all our lives
You have shown you are faithful to the end

At one Vineyard service that I attended, we sang a praise chorus calling for breaking down "dividing walls" between men and women, fathers and their children, and young and old and becoming one in the Lord. We also sang about breaking down dividing walls between traditions: We're not Baptist, not Vineyard, not Presbyterians or Lutherans. We are Christians, one in the Lord (a close paraphrase of the lyrics).

Most of the music is played and sung in contemporary musical idioms. Soft rock is the preferred style in many churches. At New Song hard rock, rap, and a modified form of grunge can be heard, but I also heard there a lovely rendition of Bach's "Jesus, Joy of Man's Desiring," using a guitar and keyboard as the lead instruments. The latter was a striking example of retraditioning, clothing an older musical form in contemporary garb. One large Lutheran congregation, the Community of Joy in Phoenix, Arizona, even has a country-and-western service with the pastoral leaders conducting the service in boots, vest, and a western string tie.

Clapping, swaying, lifting of hands, and sometimes dancing may accompany the singing. At a service in one of the Vineyard congregations, I watched a young man dance and sway, trancelike, for almost thirty minutes as the congregation sang praise choruses.

Dress styles vary. If one wishes to dress more formally, that is all right; however, informal dress is typical—in contrast to the formal dress that one must wear daily in the corporate world. At New Song, jeans, cutoffs, and T-shirts are the norm, even for the worship leaders. Though Christian symbols are absent in most of the buildings, they are often in evidence on the T-shirts.

The one pervasive symbol that is present—and it is obviously more than a symbol in these congregations—is the Bible. Most members would not think of arriving without their well-used, well-marked Bibles, to which they refer regularly during the services. They sometimes carry them in cloth covers, which a friend calls "Bible cozies." When my wife and I attended services at the Christian Faith Center minus a Bible, we were quickly offered one by a woman across the aisle. "Next time," she told us smiling, "you can bring yours." There was hardly a page in her

Bible that did not include passages that she had highlighted with multi-colored markers.

Combined with the changes in architecture, worship spaces, music, and dress styles are other ecclesial practices: different types of worship experiences, a heavy reliance on small-group involvement, considerable emphasis on lay ministry, and expressions of mission, especially local. Some new-style churches have emulated the well-known seeker services that Willow Creek has popularized. Such services are low-key, nondemanding, and very professionally done. They include popular Christian music, dramatic skits that treat questions of faith and everyday living, and end with a short sermon or teaching, again around some everyday life situation. Video clips from contemporary films and television often illustrate sermon points. All is designed to flow smoothly and quickly and to avoid being boring. Such services are clearly intended to reach out to the restless seekers of a posttraditional society, the disembedded individuals whose identities are not tied to a particular place or people, but who stroll through the spiritual marketplace in search of meaning wherever and from whomever they can find it. The aim of the service, however, is not to encourage perpetual seeking but to lead the seeker to make a deeper commitment of his or her life to Jesus Christ; in short, to become a fully devoted follower of Christ.

To that end, Willow Creek and many of its imitators also offer at least one and sometimes two other weekly services, usually on a weeknight. This service is designed for members and others who have made a Christian commitment and want to go deeper. These services, which include periodic observances of the Lord's Supper and baptism, are heavy on teaching, usually through a sermon that is a verse-by-verse exposition of a biblical text. At Chapel Hill Bible Church, which does not have a separate seeker service, Jim Abrahamson, the church's teaching pastor, does not preach in the traditional sense of the word at any of the congregation's three Sunday morning services. Rather, he blends a conservative, verse-by-verse exposition of scripture with sophisticated cultural analysis, often tackling difficult contemporary issues.

Like Chapel Hill Bible Church, many other posttraditional congregations have also chosen not to have a separate seeker service. Instead, they blend elements of the seeker service with more traditional elements of worship, or they have two Sunday services: one contemporary in flavor, the other traditional. Similarly, new-style Catholic parishes tend not to have seeker services, but offer multiple masses that differ in worship style according to the group that typically attends.

The small-group emphasis, widely practiced in posttraditional congregations, is a way of providing smaller communities within the large congregations where highly mobile, disembedded people can experience more intimate community, establish friendships, and find guidance and support in dealing with issues that face them in their families, work experience, and other relationships. They are also primary places for spiritual growth and the experience of the sacred. God is experienced in community, not in solitary contemplation, as traditional practices of spirituality have typically emphasized. Most small groups include some Bible reading, sharing, and prayer, whatever the group's stated purpose. Many focus on marriage, family, and parenting issues. Some are twelve-step groups to help people deal with addictions. Some are for singles, others for divorcees, others for new parents. Some congregations (the Generation-X-oriented New Song Church, for example) combine older and younger members so that the older members can serve as mentors and role models for the young. New Song also has a small-group program for children who have experienced parental divorce or separation, the death of a parent, or who have been the victims of abuse—experiences that are not new but have sharply increased under detraditionalizing pressures. From the congregation's perspective, small groups are strategies for doing evangelism, pastoral care, and fostering spiritual growth toward "Fully Devoted Followers of Christ." From the members' perspective, the variety of alternatives, like a mall with its host of small shops and boutiques, provides multiple options for addressing personal needs. As with the seeker services, the groups often function on a relatively nondemanding, short-term basis. One can choose to leave the group without encountering much pressure to remain.

Most of these congregations are not isolated from their communities. They are not separatist as their fundamentalist counterparts tend to be. As noted previously, they place primary emphasis on evangelization and nurture of individuals; nevertheless, they also encourage and expect their members to be "salt and light" in the world. Although the more conservative new-style congregations typically line up on opposite sides of some social issues from their mainline counterparts, their actual community involvement is relatively similar. They sponsor food and clothing banks, organize tutoring programs, help to run homeless shelters, participate in Habitat for Humanity, and offer various twelve-step recovery groups to community residents as well as to members. A group at Willow Creek accepts donated used cars (often from members), repairs them, and gives them to families and individuals who need a car but cannot afford one. Chapel Hill Bible Church sponsors a Center for Psychological and Family Services and has recently begun an AIDS Ministry—both open to anyone in the larger community. Saint Francis Catholic Church in Raleigh, North Carolina, which exhibits many characteristics of a new-style congregation, has a staff person whose job it is to coordinate member volunteers for various community social ministries.

In all the diverse ministries of most posttraditional churches, leaders place strong emphasis on doing things well, on providing high quality programs. Leaders believe that proclaiming the gospel requires and deserves nothing less. At Willow Creek, for example, all leaders from the senior ministers to lay volunteer leaders solicit and are given regular feedback in order to improve the quality of their ministries.

Finally, even as they strive for excellence in their ministries, these nontraditional churches are high-commitment congregations. In this they are much more like their fundamentalist counterparts than typical low-demand, conventional congregations. They not only ask members to commit their time, talent, and treasure to the congregation and its ministries; they *expect* them to do so, and they have developed structured ways of realizing these expectations: new member classes are required; mentors are provided for new members; members join care groups; assistance is offered in discovering one's gifts for ministry (as noted previously, some take specialized training and become staff members); there are ministry fairs and volunteer recruitment drives to enlist members in congregational and community ministries. Willow Creek asks its members to renew their commitment annually; those who do not renew their commitment are dropped from the rolls. Studies of several of these churches show that at least half of the members are weekly attenders, a figure that is considerably higher than for mainline congregations, where a percentage in the mid-to-low 30s is more normal. Members of these churches give regularly and generously and are involved in various ministries in the church or community.[15] Obviously, however, if 50 percent are highly committed, then another 50 percent are less committed in varying degrees. Not all want the high commitment that is expected. Willow Creek's leaders worry at times that too many participants in the seeker services seem content to allow these services to be the extent of their involvement.

One study of megachurches by sociologist Scott Thumma (1996: 454) suggests that the relatively large number of less involved members—"free riders" as they are sometimes called—may, however, actually be an asset in ways that they are not for smaller congregations. Too many "free riders" in smaller churches leave the congregation dependent on the contributions of time and money of a relatively small pool of members. In contrast, "free riders" in megachurches provide a "critical mass" of worshipers Sunday after Sunday that helps to attract others to the church. As Thumma says, "Large numbers help the church to stand out in the religious marketplace." If such large numbers are attending, even if they are not heavily involved in congregational life, then something interesting and exciting must be happening.

African-American Variations

Before concluding this discussion of posttraditional congregations, I want also to take note of the growth of similar types of congregations among African-Americans. Although much that I have described is characteristic of predominantly black as well as white congregations, there are important ways in which African-American churches differ from their white counterparts that are especially pertinent to my focus on processes of detraditionalization.

Because of the continuing power of the African-American cultural heritage, including its religious heritage, which helped blacks survive years of slavery and a century of official and unofficial segregation,[16] African-American traditions remain somewhat strong. Although slavery was the ultimate detraditionalizing experience, traditions developed in the midst of slavery and forced segregation, including survivals of African traditions, continue to provide important roots for African-American identity. The black church has been a major carrier of these traditions, and it has remained a central institution for African-Americans. At the same time, however, a growing number of black young adults—Baby Boomers and Generation Xers—have achieved middle-class status as a result of the Civil Rights struggles. They have college degrees, good jobs, and homes in the suburbs; and they experience many of the same detraditionalizing, disembedding pressures that their white counterparts face: fragmentation, choices, consumerism, and pluralism.

These two characteristics, the continuing power of the African-American religious tradition and the significant growth of a younger black middle class, have been contributors to the development of a number of posttraditional African-American congregations that reflect both characteristics. Among such congregations are Bethel African Methodist Episcopal (A.M.E.) Church in Baltimore;[17] Friendship Missionary Baptist Church in Charlotte; First and Ward A.M.E. Churches, both in Los Angeles; Windsor Village United Methodist Church in Houston; and St. Luke "Community" United Methodist Church and Concord Missionary Baptist Church in Dallas, to mention but a few. These are congregations that honor and celebrate the African-American religious heritage, but they also attempt to speak to the new detraditionalizing realities of corporate and suburban life that the growing black middle class faces. In doing so, they provide roots, a haven from the white world, and assistance in addressing the issues that they confront daily.

Some, like Bethel and Ward, or the Christian Faith Center near Durham, North Carolina, add a neo-Pentecostal dimension that emphasizes lively, Spirit-filled worship led by instrumentalists and professional-quality gospel singing groups. Healing services and speaking in tongues are part of the experience of worshipers at the Christian Faith Center. At Bethel and Ward, neo-Pentecostalism includes honoring aspects of the black religious folk tradition such as shouting and being overcome by the Spirit. Bethel also celebrates its African heritage in a large mural on the back wall of the chancel that shows black Christians around the base of the cross. While not neo-Pentecostal, both Friendship Missionary Baptist and St. Luke also celebrate the black religious heritage. Their sanctuaries have stained glass windows depicting various African-American saints such as Martin Luther King Jr., Malcolm X, and Sojourner Truth.

Along with the emphasis on the black heritage, these congregations offer multiple high-quality programs: Bible study and other small groups, choirs, young adult programs for singles and marrieds, youth and children's programs, and a host of opportunities for lay involvement in ministries both to the church community and to the larger community around the church. At Bethel, for example, community ministries address needs of women, unwed teen mothers, drug addicts, homeless people, ex-convicts, prisoners, students, senior citizens, and the deaf (Mamiya 1994: 276).

These African-American posttraditional congregations are therefore like their predominantly white counterparts in size, lively worship and music, and the use of high-quality, professionally done programs to address members' multiple interests and needs. But, unlike the predominantly white churches, most do not downplay at least one powerful tradition: the African-American religious heritage. This tradition still anchors black Americans, who experience various detraditionalizing pressures along with persisting racism.

Summary Reflections

In this chapter, I have described a number of ways in which religious groups, particularly congregations, are responding to unsettling, detraditionalizing processes. Some, especially fundamentalists, attempt quite self-consciously to resist detraditionalization; others, like Sheila Larson or many small-group participants, accommodate to it in varying degrees. Yet others have borrowed from both sides of the resistance-accommodation continuum, especially the posttraditional congregations that I have profiled in some detail. I could obviously mention other examples, though perhaps these are sufficient to make my point: what these ecclesial responses, especially posttraditional congregations, represent are efforts to create innovative strategies of action—beliefs, rituals, symbols, and practices—for unsettled times.

Posttraditional church strategies are at neither extreme of the continuum between resistance and accommodation. They are neither sectarian nor mystical in the Troeltschian sense. Instead they exhibit elements of both. In their response to detraditionalization they have drawn together a cultural tool kit that includes biblical sources and practices, symbols and practices from the corporate world, and the symbols and styles of contemporary popular culture. The result is a spiritual and material congregational culture that in most respects stands in striking contrast to conventional congregations. These churches practice what some have called bricolage, mixing codes and symbols from various sources, but their overriding aim is to give the church a place at the table in a posttraditional world.

As a way of summing up the dominant characteristics of these congregations, I list their major strategies of action that, when taken together, describe a posttraditional ecclesial style:

- their large size, in contrast to the majority of traditional Protestant congregations;
- a willingness to leapfrog centuries of tradition, while claiming biblical precedent for their innovations;
- theological conservatism without being fundamentalist (majoring in the majors);
- the lack of formal denominational ties (characteristic of some), or, if denominationally related, a willingness to sit lightly to these ties;
- strong, entrepreneurial leadership, often supported by internally trained staff specialists, and coupled with considerable emphasis on lay exercise of spiritual gifts—all in a framework that minimizes hierarchy and distance between clergy and laity;

- intentionality of purpose, especially in identifying and seeking ways to address a target audience;
- commitment to leading their constituents to become "Fully Devoted Followers of Christ";
- buildings that lack the look and feel of traditional churches and that are located to draw broadly from a region rather than to service a particular local community;
- avoidance of most traditional and classical forms of church music in favor of forms that reflect contemporary musical tastes;
- informal dress styles, often for the clergy as well as for the laity;
- low-key, nondemanding, professionally done worship services—some in the seeker service style of Willow Creek;
- heavy reliance on small-group ministries designed to respond to the issues and needs of a consumer culture but also to provide the warmth, intimacy, mutual support, and accountability that are also valued and important in developing mature Christians;
- opportunities for members to become involved in outreach ministries, primarily at the local community level;
- high commitment expectations for those who become members, along with a commitment to excellence in ministries by their leaders.

Taken together, this list of characteristics and practices signals a distinctive ecclesial style: multiple and innovative strategies of action that have emerged as an adaptive response to the challenges of a detraditionalizing society. They stand in rather striking contrast to conventional, mainstream congregations.

The list also makes clear that posttraditional congregations have taken the participatory congregations described by Brooks Holifield (see chapter 1) to a new level. Laity take increasing initiative in defining the terms for their involvement in congregations—and are encouraged to do so by their leaders—rather than acquiescing to clergy dictates or following uncritically patterns handed down from the past. In responding to what they perceive to be the interests and desires of their potential constituents—their target market—these congregations downplay traditions: denominational, liturgical, musical, and architectural. From their perspective, traditions are perhaps appropriate for settled times, giving people a secure sense of continuity with the past and an identity in the present. But these are unsettled times, and they call for innovative new strategies, which, like the ecclesial practices described in the Acts of the Apostles, are believed to be Spirit-directed. What results is a distinctly horizontal, present-oriented ecclesial style that contrasts sharply with the ecclesial styles of more traditional churches.

However one feels about these congregations (and they can be faulted theologically at many points), they represent a serious effort by religious innovators to come to grips with the unsettling characteristics of a posttraditional society, and they have spoken with considerable success to the religious and spiritual hunger of the generations most affected by posttraditional society—the Baby Boomers and Busters. My question is this: Can those who lead or are members of more traditional congregations (or who, like myself, teach in theological seminaries) learn from these innovators without swallowing the whole cake? Do they suggest ways that can help those in more traditional churches to reframe reflectively their own ecclesial practices to be more faithful and effective as God's people in a posttraditional society?

In chapter 1, I cited some words of Karl Barth, including his observation that there has never been any "intrinsically sacred sociology [of the church.]" I am fairly certain that Barth would not have approved of many of the strategies of action that I have described. I believe, however, that he would have applauded the intent of finding new ways of fulfilling the church's calling to be the people of God in the world.

3

Tradition, Freedom, and the Challenge of Posttraditional Congregations

Tradition means giving votes to the most obscure of all classes—our ancestors. It is the democracy of the dead. Tradition refuses to submit to the small and arrogant oligarchy of those who merely happen to be walking around.

G. K. Chesterton (1909)

Wasn't church a lot easier when God didn't show up? Then you knew what time you would get home for Sunday dinner.

Preacher at Vineyard "Catch the Fire" Service

An article in a newspaper in Portland, Oregon (O'Keefe 1996), focused on the membership losses of mainline denominations and commented: "The seven sister mainline denominations . . . could go the way of the dinosaur if they don't change quickly to meet the needs of the changing spiritual landscape. When surveys show grave concern about the nation's moral climate, people, especially the young, aren't turning to the traditional religious institutions that once defined America like a Norman Rockwell painting." Reading this led me to respond, "So what's new?" Newspapers have chronicled the plight of mainline churches for the past twenty-five years. Hardly a month passes without an article on the topic. I cite the quotation, however, because of its pertinence to the theme of these chapters, especially where I left off in chapter 2. Does the mainline have a future, and if so, can it change to meet the needs of the changing spiritual landscape? What are the challenges and lessons of the posttraditional churches and other new forms of local ecclesiologies in the change process?

Are those of us in mainline churches at a point where we must jettison familiar ecclesial traditions by which we have ordered our congregational life and practices over the centuries in order to engage in ministry and mission in a posttraditional society? That, in large part, is the assumption of many who are scrambling to emulate the posttraditional congregations, adopting their strategies of action and discarding traditional practices. The *necessity* of doing so is the message that church consultants such as Lyle Schaller are preaching. Adding specificity to the newspaper's prognosis, Schaller (1996: 26) predicts that over one hundred thousand congregations will choose dissolution in the next five decades because they will be unwilling to make the necessary changes, which, for him, are best represented by the strategies pioneered by entrepreneurial leaders of posttraditional congregations.

Schaller combines theological and pragmatic reasons in making this judgment. Theologically, he argues that the church that refuses to change is ignoring Jesus' Great Commission to "go therefore and make disciples of all nations, baptizing them in the name of the Father and of the Son and of the Holy Spirit, and teaching them to obey everything that I have commanded you" (Matthew 28:19–20). Pragmatically, as Schaller reads the signs of the times, he believes that most mainline churches organize their life and practices in ways that appeal primarily to the generations born before 1955. For these generations, characteristics such as kinship ties, nationality, language, racial heritage, inherited denominational loyalties, geographical convenience, what the church offered their children, and doctrinal stance were important in choosing a church. For the generations born since 1955, Schaller (1996: 31) maintains that three criteria are of utmost importance: relevance to one's personal and spiritual journey, the quality of all aspects of ministry, and credibility (a congregation that practices what it preaches). These criteria, he argues, are best exemplified in the posttraditional churches, which have been willing to adapt their practices to meet the changed interests of the younger generation.

On the other side of the argument are a number of critics, some of whom come from within the evangelical movement. An article in the evangelical journal *Christianity Today,* reporting an interview with Willow Creek's founding pastor, Bill Hybels, was given the not-too-flattering title: "Selling Out the House of God?" (Maudlin and Gilbreath 1994). Although the article includes a lengthy interview with Hybels in

which he explains and defends Willow Creek's practices, both the article and the interview are couched in terms of criticisms leveled at
Hybels and other posttraditional church pastors by fellow evangelicals,
for example, theologian David Wells. In the article, Wells is quoted as
asserting that pastors such as Hybels mistakenly view the culture from
which seekers come as neutral. He wonders—in sharp contrast to
Schaller's perspective—if megachurches like Willow Creek are not
"obsequiously prostrating [themselves] before baby boomers, a generally self-centered, relativistic, unloyal generation," in their efforts to
adapt the Christian faith to Boomer culture. "The problem is," he
argues, "that culture is laden with values that inevitably go against the
thrust of the gospel message" (Maudlin and Gilbreath 1994: 23–24). In
his book *No Place for Truth, or, Whatever Happened to Evangelical
Theology* (1993: 144–45), Wells levels an attack on what he calls the
"selfism" or hypersubjectivity characteristic of contemporary culture.
"Selfism" makes the self and individual experience the measure of truth.
For the Christian, Wells maintains, truth is found not subjectively in the
self but objectively in "God's pronouncements about the meaning of life
as the only true measure" (1993: 184).

Among other critics, perhaps the most energetic (and often shrill)
have been some liturgical scholars and professional church musicians,
especially those who have participated in the joint Catholic and (mainline) Protestant liturgical renewal movement of the last quarter century
or so. Their efforts to mine the historic traditions of the church and to
rekindle use of traditional liturgical and music practices are severely
challenged by the new-style churches. One critic from this camp accuses
these churches and their leaders of a "deep disregard for the past and
alienation from tradition . . . , and this reflects the attitude of large segments of the population in our scientific, high-tech, and present-oriented
society" (Schattauer 1994: 13). What disturbs these critics is that the
church's cherished traditions are being ignored. Marva Dawn, a neo-
conservative liturgical theologian and church musician, offers an extensive critique of posttraditional church worship practices in a book with
the interesting title, *Reaching Out without Dumbing Down* (1995). Dawn
is especially critical of seeker-friendly services, praise choruses, topical
sermons, and the like, which she views as a sellout to a self-centered
culture, much in the same vein as Wells, whom she cites liberally.
Although Dawn offers constructive proposals to help the church adapt
its worship practices to a posttraditional society, she argues that God, not
the self, must be both subject and object of worship. For her, as with
Wells, truth is not found subjectively in the self but objectively in God's

self-revelation: "In the midst of a culture that has lost a sense of objective truth, the Church worships a God who can be objectively known" (Dawn 1995: 86). It is this sense of objectivity that Dawn believes is lost in the worship practices of many posttraditional congregations.

These two sides—supporters like Schaller and critics such as Wells, Dawn, and many liturgical scholars—are sharply divided: one emphasizing the need for openness to new strategies of action, jettisoning the tradition if need be, if congregations are to be faithful to the Great Commission in an unsettled, detraditionalized society; the other emphasizing the need for plumbing the historic traditions for resources, as one liturgical scholar put it, "to shape a distinctly Christian and churchly identity in response to the forces of social disintegration and theological confusion that permeate contemporary life" (Schattauer 1994: 3). For Wells and Dawn, the latter involves claiming the objective truth of the Christian revelation as a standpoint for worship and congregational life.

It is little wonder that some have referred to this conflict as a "worship war"! Extending the conflict beyond worship to other ecclesiological matters, Schaller argues that we are witnessing a battle between European hierarchical models of the church and what he calls "made in America" models. The former, he argues, are based on trust in institutions and their top leaders, and a corresponding distrust of local congregations and laity. The latter he describes as voluntary associations of mostly younger adults who say that they are following "the leading of the Holy Spirit, Jesus Christ, Scripture, [themselves], and those individuals who have earned [their] trust" (Schaller 1996: 45, 51). They sit lightly to inherited church traditions, claiming instead to base their ecclesial practices on biblical models. In short, it is a conflict between tradition and freedom, or, as some like Schaller would put it, between tradition and the leading of the Spirit. The two epigraphs at the head of this chapter reflect the conflicting points of view: Chesterton willing to give his "votes" to tradition and scornful of the "small and arrogant oligarchy of those who merely happen to be walking around"; and the Vineyard preacher who implies that conventional churches have substituted tradition for God's active presence through the Holy Spirit.

In the remainder of this chapter, I propose to examine the conflict between adherence to the church's traditions and the freedom to ignore those traditions under the leading of the Holy Spirit, in order to make the gospel culturally relevant. There is no easy or simple resolution to this conflict, but I believe that seeing what is at stake on either side of the battle is critical to being faithful to the calling to be God's people. I try also to suggest a way through this impasse that offers clues for ways congregations can respond in these unsettled times. Although it may seem somewhat ironic to do so, I want to look at the conflict by calling on the traditions of the church, especially scripture, to aid understanding.

Tradition and Freedom: New Testament Perspectives

"Hard- or soft-core" primitivists and restorationists, those who seek to leapfrog the traditions and go back to the Bible to find a single, pure New Testament blueprint for the church, will be hard-pressed to find only one such blueprint unless, as they typically do, they ignore or reinterpret the multiple ecclesiological practices present in the New Testament. Various biblical scholars such as Eduard Schweizer (1961) and Raymond Brown (1984) have shown that there is not one but many models of the church and ecclesial practices in the New Testament. There was simply no one way that the early Christians ordered their communities. They had several tool kits from which to draw. Although they drew much from their Jewish heritage, they also borrowed from Hellenistic sources; and, especially, they innovated—sometimes in a hit-or-miss style—as they faced new challenges to discover what it meant to be faithful to the gospel. Several examples make this clear. When the apostles found the demands of preaching so heavy that they did not have time to distribute food to needy widows, they called together the community to appoint deacons for the task (Acts 6:1–7), thus creating what was later to become a new order of ministry. Confronted with the challenge of the conversion of Cornelius, a Gentile, Peter, had to decide whether to baptize him along with his friends and relatives without first requiring them to be circumcised. Under the leading of the Spirit, he did so—a major innovation that left some of Peter's entourage shaking their heads (Acts 10). When opportunities for mission opened elsewhere, the Antioch church, again led by the Spirit, commissioned Barnabas and Saul as missionaries (Acts 13:1–4). Thus the churches borrowed from the practices of both Judaism and the surrounding Hellenistic culture, and they innovated, bequeathing us not one but multiple models of church order and ecclesial practice. One important way that the models differ is along lines not unlike the conflict that I am examining: the tension between adherence to established traditions and acting in freedom in the belief that innovation is following the leading of the Holy Spirit. This conflict was present in the beginning, in New Testament congregations' efforts to shape their common life and practices in response to changing circumstances.

The Argument for Tradition

Those on the tradition and order side of the conflict claim that the church lives by virtue of what God has done in the past, in the life, death, and resurrection of Jesus, and, to extend it further back, to God's dealings with the people of Israel. That is, the church is called to live in faithfulness to its past. It lives out of the story of God's action in Jesus Christ, who, furthermore, is the fulfillment of God's covenant with Israel. That narrative—that tradition—and the events to which it witnesses give shape and direction to the church's order, its practices, and its service in every age. It is not surprising that this included borrowing a number of Jewish practices, including the synagogue form of gathering. Although several New Testament books reflect this perspective in varying degrees and with important differences, its fullest expression is in the Pastoral Epistles. There the church's task is to preserve at all costs the truth of the apostolic witness against radical and heretical ideas and teachers, especially Gnostics. The writer of the epistles, claiming the authority of Paul, counsels Timothy: "Hold to the standard of sound teaching that you have heard from me, in the faith and love that are in Christ Jesus. Guard the good treasure entrusted to you, with the help of the Holy Spirit living in us" (2 Timothy 1:13–14). In modern terminology, "Don't dumb it down!" To insure faithfulness to the tradition, he also lays down guidelines for church order, including the characteristics of officeholders who are entrusted with passing on the tradition. Those guidelines themselves became part of the tradition. As Raymond Brown (1984: 39) has written, "Already the 'Paul' of the Pastorals had divined that the best response to a plethora of views claiming to be revealed and even traditional was a pedigreed tradition, involving a link between the apostolic era and approved church officials."

The Argument for Freedom

Equally strong is another emphasis: that of the church living in the immediacy and freedom of the Spirit. The church looks not to the past but instead to experiences of fellowship with its living and exalted Lord. One does not need to look back to past events or ahead to some future fulfillment. Instead members of the community regularly meet the risen Christ and participate now in God's reign. It is especially the case as they gather at the table for the Lord's Supper, and as members experience now the gifts and guidance of the Holy Spirit. It is in the Johannine communities that this particular understanding of the church finds its clearest expression. Especially in contrast to the Pastorals with their emphasis on the apostolic tradition and a hierarchy of bishops, elders, and deacons, John's congregations are eminently egalitarian. Every Christian is a disciple by virtue of his or her immediate relationship with Jesus through the Holy Spirit. Even if there are officeholders, as implied in Jesus' post-resurrection encounter with Peter (probably a later addition to John's Gospel), they are to exercise loving, shepherding care after the model of the Good Shepherd. The officeholder is not a guardian of the tradition. That is the job of the Holy Spirit, who is a living teacher of what Jesus has said and done and who makes that teaching contemporary so that the community can face new situations that arise: "I still have many things to say to you, but you cannot bear them now," Jesus tells the disciples. "When the Spirit of truth comes, he will guide you into all the truth; for he will not speak on his own, but will speak whatever he hears, and he will declare to you the things that are to come" (John 16:12–13).

Movement or Institution?

This tension between faithfulness to the tradition and living in the freedom of the Holy Spirit is not restricted to New Testament congregations. It is an age-old tension that was present earlier in the Old Testament and, in truth, has been with us throughout the history of the church. The tension can be expressed in the following questions: Does the life of the covenant people have the character of an event of grace in response to God's call that takes the form of a social movement? Or is it an institution, with settled practices and a stable order? In a discussion of ecclesiology, Colin Williams (1968: 26ff.) calls attention to the Abraham and Moses motifs as symbolic of these two social modes. Abraham, he says, symbolizes the "event" character of the people of God that is characteristic of a *movement*. Abraham went out giving up all securities, stretching out beyond that which was institutionally given, in obedience to the call of God. His call, like that of the people of God in all times, is an event of grace. In contrast, Moses symbolizes an *institutional* form of social organization. He received the law from God, also an event of grace, but with it he also received a rich institutional life for ordering Israel's life. Israel was still called to live as a pilgrim people, but in the law and cult they were given (or developed) traditions, a characteristic style and form, to guide them on their pilgrim journey. These institutionalized traditions set boundaries on their existence as a people. Williams notes that, although these two motifs are ultimately complementary, they are also in severe tension, at times reaching a breaking point.

Over a millennium later, the breaking point was reached for Luther, Calvin, and other Reformers when they could no longer remain within the institutional boundaries of the medieval Catholic Church, nor would the Methodist movement stay within the bounds of the Anglican Church, in spite of Wesley's hope that it could avoid a break by renewing the institution from within. Most of the Reformers, however, were not leaders of radical movements. While affirming *sola scriptura,* they did not abandon the tradition; rather, they jettisoned or changed what they saw as its abuses. And they fairly quickly established new institutions and traditions. In contrast, Thomas Münzer and others of the left wing of the Reformation were more clearly on the movement side in their break with the institutional church.

Closer to our own time and place, a similar conflict between these two motifs would break out again, this time following the American Revolution, a period of significant unsettledness. It was also a time of considerable innovation. Democratizing impulses led "upstart sects," as they have been called—especially Baptists, Methodists, and Disciples of Christ—to challenge the tradition-based practices of the established colonial churches—Presbyterians, Congregationalists, and Episcopalians. Nathan Hatch, in *The Democratization of American Christianity,* has masterfully chronicled the movement-building enterprise of these upstart groups, to which he also added the black churches and Mormons. "Each was led by young men of relentless energy who went about movement-building as self-conscious outsiders. They shared an ethic of unrelenting toil, a passion for expansion, a hostility to orthodox belief and style, a zeal for religious reconstruction, and a systematic plan to realize their ideals" (Hatch 1989: 4).

These new groups adopted a populist, "movement" style ecclesiology in contrast to the established "institutionalist" ecclesiology characterized by an educated clergy and ecclesial practices reflecting the high culture of the day. Among the strategies of action that they developed were the often raucous, high-voltage camp meetings as a primary tool of evangelism. Circuit-riding preachers stood in sharp contrast to the practice of settled ministries of the older churches; and these itinerants left behind lay-led class meetings as they traveled, an early form of small-group ministry aimed at maturing new disciples. The upstarts also pioneered a colloquial, storytelling style of preaching, and they borrowed lively, easy-to-sing, popular tunes—folk songs, ballads, and black spirituals—to express their faith and fervor. In these and other ways, they exhibited a movement ecclesiology, much to the distress of critics, who preferred more traditional ecclesial institutions and practices.

Sociologically speaking, the contrast between institutions and movements signals two important forms of association. Institutions are asso-
ciational patterns and practices that have been infused or endowed with
value. They have a binding character, in large measure as a result of the
traditions they embody. In contrast, movements are much more fluid
and free-floating associations, much more given to spontaneity and
change. Of course traditions and institutions are, themselves, rarely static. They must be renewed and reinterpreted—retraditioned—as new
circumstances arise, or they die. Likewise movements rarely persist
over time without becoming institutionalized or stabilized. They
develop their own guiding narratives and traditions. The experiences,
perspectives, roles, and practices that the movement develops become
themselves infused with value: a canon of sacred texts is established;
roles that were fluid and functional become formal offices; liturgical
practices become routinized and fixed. In time, this process of institutionalization may give rise to a new movement, a new protest against
the old movement that has become hardened into an institutional form.

Max Weber (1968: 1111–57) referred to this process as the "routinization of charisma." After the initial charismatic period, often at the
death of a movement's founder or founders, the movement undergoes
routinization. Leadership struggles may ensue. Efforts are made to preserve the teachings and practices that the founder initiated. Hatch's
telling of the story of the upstart sects illustrates Weber's point well.
What he calls "the allure of respectability dampened the original fire of
the religious populists. Many second-generation Baptists, Methodists,
and Disciples yearned to recover a place of influence and respect"
(Hatch 1989: 195). So they gave up circuit riding for a settled ministry.
They built more elaborate church buildings, toned down the religious
fervor and spontaneity of their worship, developed centralized denominational structures, and established educational institutions that would
provide a more learned clergy—much to the consternation of some
leaders who believed that these forms of institutionalization or routinization would have dire consequences for the church's mission.[1]

My point in making these contrasts is to emphasize that the current
conflict between the practices of more traditional congregations and
those of posttraditional forms of the church has many similarities to tensions that are present in scripture and church history. And these tensions
are examples of broader sociological tensions between movements and
institutions in many areas of life beyond the church. Most of our mainline Protestant churches and most Catholic parishes fall clearly on the
institutional or traditional pole. We order our congregational practices in

terms of valued ways of "being church" that have come to us out of our denominational and Christian past. They are familiar to us; we cherish them; we feel comfortable with them. They are how church is supposed to be and feel. Stephen Warner (1988: 35–36) captures our mainline institutional practices in his study of a Presbyterian congregation in Mendocino, California, appropriately titled *New Wine in Old Wineskins:*

> Consider the typical downtown Protestant church. People wear their Sunday best to attend services on a holy day in a sacred place. Within the sacred place, some spaces are more sacred than others, the altar, for example. Leadership in worship is monopolized by religious professionals, whose supramundane attire is a badge of their status. They speak with an intonation that would sound strange outside the sacred walls, and they follow a formal and explicit order of worship. They treat the religious artifacts—the pulpit Bible, the cross, the communion elements, the offering plate—with solemn respect. Aside from any words that are uttered in such an hour of worship, the entire ritual itself expresses the idea of the persistence and majesty of an extraordinary reality, the sacred world, which is set off from the business of this world, the secular world.

These traditional practices, of course, are not static. They are regularly clarified and reinterpreted as we face new circumstances, both at the local congregational level and denominationally. The ordination of women and the introduction of new liturgical practices are two prime examples. Both contradict existing traditions in order to take account of new contexts—the feminist movement on the one hand and the ecumenical movement on the other. Yet we continue to value existing traditions and familiar ways of doing things, changing them only with great difficulty, as conflicts that have arisen over extending ordination to women or changing our familiar liturgies make clear. Though we profess belief in *ecclesia semper reformanda*, we do so mostly in moderation, "decently and in order," as Presbyterians are fond of saying. Some Catholics joke that if Jesus returned for the second coming and tried to change anything, the pope would cite tradition for why this would not be possible; but such traditionalism is clearly not restricted to Presbyterians and Catholics.

In contrast to traditional congregations, new-style or posttraditional churches fall toward the movement or "Spirit" pole. Here is Warner's characterization of a movement-style religious group—in this case a countercultural group (the "new wine" of his title)—that transformed Mendocino Presbyterian Church:

> Those in the nascent state [Warner's designation for Spirit-directed movements] . . . refuse to acknowledge a special place for religion, for their claims are more radical than those of the institutional church. They adopt symbols that fuse sacred and secular, where guitars are as godly as organs, Ritz crackers suffice for communion, and everyday speech is used to address God. Their meetings seem to be less orderly than the services in the institutional church, and that is partly due to the much greater proportion of the members who take a leading role in the proceedings. The experience itself proclaims the continuity of sacred and secular life: nothing is innocent of religion.

Warner's description of "nascent" or movement congregational styles, with notable exceptions, is an apt portrayal of several important characteristics of posttraditional congregations.[2] These congregations are much more movement-like in their practices than are traditional mainline congregations. To be sure, these newer congregations are rapidly developing institutional characteristics, such as their growing tendency to look alike, to emulate the successful models, and to form themselves into associations that are beginning to look like denominations. My guess is that they will continue on the path toward institutionalization, and at some time in the future they will be challenged by new movements that criticize their "traditionalism." Nevertheless, they currently have considerably more in common with the Johannine communities than they do with the communities to whom the Pastoral Epistles were addressed. An obvious major exception is that some of these congregations refuse to accept the ordination of women, and they turn to the Pastoral Epistles for justification. In general, however, they sit loosely to traditions and emphasize the immediacy of the believer's personal experience of Jesus through the workings of the Holy Spirit. They blur distinctions between the sacred and the secular—in music and architecture, for example. Although the congregations have strong pastoral leadership, they, like the Johannine communities, also blur distinctions between clergy and laity. All members are not only encouraged but expected to exercise their gifts for ministry.

Combining Tradition and Freedom

What then are we to make of these competing local ecclesiologies? Are the conflicts between tradition and freedom in the Spirit or between institutions and movements irreconcilable? Without minimizing the differences, I want to argue that they are not. To do so, let me return to the

New Testament communities. Although there were severe tensions between tradition-oriented and Spirit-led communities that resulted in serious splits, especially in the second century, both orientations were present, if dialectically so, in most of the early congregations. This was true especially for the Pauline communities.

On the side of tradition, the Pauline congregations were brought into being by an apostle, and they were under his authority. Frequently, rather than citing particular precepts, Paul simply cited what was for him the core tradition that formed the heart of his preaching. He framed it in various ways, using differing images that carried similar meanings: "Jesus Christ, and him crucified" (1 Corinthians 2:2); or "Christ Jesus, who died, yes, who was raised, who is at the right hand of God" (Romans 8:34); or "Jesus died and rose again" (1 Thessalonians 4: 14).[3] Jesus' story, especially his death and resurrection, constituted for Paul the core of the tradition. But Paul also cited other traditions as circumstances dictated. At one point, after scolding the Corinthian congregation for a variety of practices that reflected their immature faith and understanding, he commends them "because you remember me in everything and maintain the traditions just as I handed them on to you" (1 Corinthians 11:2). In this case, the tradition seems to refer to practices already established (institutionalized) in other Christian communities or in synagogue traditions. Some of those traditions, I am grateful, we have seen fit to discard. So Paul was not averse to citing both his core tradition or these lesser traditions as they were needed. His dual use of tradition illustrates the distinction made above in chapter 1 between *traditio* (the core message of the tradition) and *traditum* (adaptations of the core, in Paul's case sometimes borrowed from other traditions).

At the same time, Paul's teaching also emphasizes the "event" character of the church. Members of the community are already, through the Spirit, one in Christ and radically equal: equally sinful, but equally recipients of God's grace; equally members of Christ's body, and equally sharing in the gifts of the Spirit for the good of the whole; equally free *from* the constraints of the law, yet at the same time equally free and responsible *for* that which builds up the community. In the emphasis on spiritual gifts, offices in the Pauline congregations seem not to have been fixed and hierarchical, but functional and fluid. It is important to note, however, that Paul never called Christians to exercise their freedom in ways that would have violated the core of his preaching: "Jesus Christ and him crucified." One can paraphrase Augustine's famous dictum, "Love God and do as you please." For Paul it was "Honor Jesus Christ and him crucified, and do as you please."

This combination of tradition and freedom, of institutional order and the event character of a movement, allowed Paul to emphasize one or the other side of the dialectic as circumstances dictated. On the one hand, against prevailing cultural traditions concerning males and females, rich and poor, slave and free, Jew and Gentile, he came down on the side of freedom in the Spirit, emphasizing the radical equality that comes from being "one in Christ Jesus" here and now (Galatians 3:28). The same was true concerning the law: "now that faith has come, we are no longer subject to a disciplinarian, for in Christ Jesus you are all children of God through faith" (Galatians 3:25–26). On the other hand, when freedom was abused and the congregations threatened to turn into radical individualists, or when they engaged in manifestly immature or sinful behavior, or when they faced the challenges of how to live as Christians in a pagan environment and were in danger of accommodating to it, Paul did not hesitate to come down on the side of tradition, drawing on tradition(s) to shape and guide the beliefs, behavior, and practices of the community. One might think of Paul's interpretive strategy as an early example of reflexivity—redefining situations and acting in light of experience in ways that did not violate the core of his faith.

In other early Christian communities—for example, the churches to whom the Pastorals were addressed or the Johannine community—the dialectic between tradition and freedom was not as strongly maintained. When they clearly emphasized one or the other side, it was often because heretical movements of one sort or another or abuses in the church threatened them.

> When, in the face of the menace of gnostic fanaticism, there was a danger that the gospel would disintegrate into something timeless and unhistorical, and the Church into a sum total of religious individualists, the Church's historicity, tradition, and order had to be stressed; and that was done in the Pastorals. But with the threat of an institutional Church, in which a monarchical bishop wanted to rule everything, the self-sufficiency of the Church as it stood under the living activity of the Holy Spirit had to be stressed; and this was done in the Johannine churches (Schweizer 1961: 168).

So we have a dialectic of tradition and freedom as a legacy from the earliest days of the church. Although I risk confusing the issue, let me suggest that each side of the dialectic is a part of our tradition; or, to avoid confusion, we can call each of them a primary narrative. One is a narrative that emphasizes order, institutions, and tradition; the other a narrative stressing freedom and movement. Both are present in scripture, and both are present in the history of the church, often as competing but complementary narratives.[4] Nevertheless, although they differ in important ways, both are part of our heritage; both are concerned with how congregations order their common life and practices to participate in the continuing ministry of Jesus Christ; and both witness to the "one Lord, one faith, one baptism, one God and Father of us all" (Ephesians 4:5).

Maintaining the dialectic between these two narratives, between tradition and freedom, is never easy. Rarely are they in balance. Circumstances often dictate otherwise. My central point is that the circumstances of posttraditional society call for us to come down on the side of freedom and boldness in adapting existing ecclesial practices to meet the new realities and, at times, in constructing new practices. This is what it means to live reflexively—open to new ways of being faithful to the gospel that are appropriate to the new context in which we live.

To say this is not a call to forget or ignore the church's traditions, but to heed Barth's words that there is no sacred sociology of the church. Although he recognized the necessity and importance of church order, Barth saw the church's forms as relative and provisional, open to change and reconstruction in the service of the church's primary task as witness to the "Yes" of God to humankind. Elsewhere (1956: 660), he referred to the church as "an *église du désert*, . . . a 'moving tent' like the biblical tabernacle." For him, the church exists solely out of God's free grace. Paul Tillich, who differed from Barth on many points of theology, made a quite similar point when he spoke of "the Protestant principle" (Tillich 1948). This principle reflects "a living, moving, restless power" that stands in opposition to every attempt to claim absolute status for any relative reality, including church traditions or ecclesial structures.

If this is the case, then are we not free to learn from the strategies of action of the new-style congregations and others who are trying to respond to detraditionalization? We also must work to develop our own innovative strategies of action. What this might imply for us is the topic of the final chapter. For now, however, I want to ask the difficult question of how we "test the spirits" of our innovations.

Testing the Spirits

Let me stay for a moment with Barth's perspective. Given his view of the church as an event, continually called into being by Jesus Christ through the activity of the Holy Spirit, Barth rejects any ontological status for the church as the body of Christ. It is not an extension of the incarnation, as some have claimed. It cannot claim pride of being a "second Christ." Instead, it is holy only in the biblical sense that it is set apart as a peculiar people distinct from the world about it. Its holiness and peculiarity consist not in the piety or goodness of its members nor in the sanctity of its institutional forms. Rather, its holiness is tested by the degree to which it is a reflection of the holiness of Jesus Christ as he enters into fellowship with it. As the church is exposed in Word and Sacrament to Jesus' activity, it is jolted by this exposure and asked to what extent its visible life in the world corresponds to the fact that it is Christ's body.

This christological test is a crucial if difficult way of thinking about the church and especially about ecclesial practices in unsettled times. It is crucial because it reminds the church of its calling to be faithful to its core identity as Christ's body. There is a shape to Jesus' life, teachings, death, and resurrection to which the church is called to conform itself in its programs and practices. I have previously noted how Paul used a similar test when he called the Corinthians to shape their beliefs and practices according to the core tradition that he had been given: "Jesus Christ, and him crucified" (1 Corinthians 2:2). In another letter, Paul tells the Christians at Philippi: "Only, live your life in a manner worthy of the gospel of Christ" (Philippians 1:27). Although Paul was here referring primarily to the Philippians' moral lives, his words are also applicable to ecclesial practices. Let them be "worthy of the gospel of Christ." But the christological test is also quite difficult, because we have no precise guidelines for its application. While the shape and substance of Jesus' life, teachings, death, and resurrection do jolt us when we are confronted with them, it is not always a simple matter to test our practices by them. So at times we have to "sin boldly," to use Luther's phrase, not always sure how, not always certain of our faithfulness, but engaging reflectively in an ongoing dialogue between the gospel narratives and the culture in which we live, trusting the Holy Spirit to guide our exercise of freedom. This is both the challenge and the burden of Christian and ecclesial life in posttraditional society.

A Continuing Role for Tradition(s)?

But where does this leave the church's traditions? Do we ignore them? Are they no longer to be trusted as reliable guides? By no means do I want to suggest that traditions are no longer important. As congregations move into uncharted territory, they have to exercise their freedom to innovate and create new strategies of action, but they risk being unfaithful to their calling if they think that they can cut themselves off from a reflective conversation with the past or ignore the church's traditions.

The idea of a totally fresh start, free from the past, is attractive but perilous. It is exemplified in the experience of the early Christian Marcion, who was condemned by the church as a heretic for trying to persuade Christians to ignore their past. He advocated throwing out the Old Testament, keeping only the Gospel of Luke and the Pauline letters as his Bible. Although some may argue that the church would have benefited had his program succeeded—for example, we would not have to deal with many of the gory Old Testament stories involving the God whom Marcion thought to be a lesser deity than the one revealed in Jesus—the loss would have been enormous. The richness of the Old Testament, including Israel's struggles to understand God and God's ways, as well as the church's identity as rooted in these struggles, would be lost.[5] Similarly, were we today simply to ignore the various Christian traditions in which we stand, we would be much the poorer. Many of them continue to convey truth and wisdom appropriate to the present. As Edward Farley (1996: 32) has written, "History . . . is not simply a sequence of utterly dissociated moments, each one having no connection to the previous one. . . . Thus, the particular way southeast Asian Buddhism experiences and interprets suffering may offer a wisdom to peoples very different than southeast Asians." The same can be said of the various strands of Christian tradition that come to us from quite different periods of history from our own. Thus it may be helpful to reflect further about the meaning and continuing role of tradition.

When I introduced the term "posttraditional" as a description of the social and cultural world in which we now live, I indicated that it overstates the case if it is taken to mean the end of tradition. Traditions have clearly not disappeared or lost their importance. Rather they have taken on a different roles in these unsettled times. Because their authority is no longer "out there," external to us, traditions of all sorts, including the church's traditions, no longer carry the objective, external authority that they once did. We may acknowledge them as authorities; we may choose to believe or practice what they teach or prescribe; but it is precisely the point of a detraditionalized world that we *choose* to acknowledge them, that we *choose* to follow them. Although this may, in principle, always have been the case, many people in the past did not see it that way. Most believed that authority was inherent in the traditions themselves, irrespective of one's decision to recognize their authority. Some, including some critics of posttraditional churches, continue to believe that today. Others do not, myself included, even if they believe, as I also do, that the churches' traditions are a precious and crucial resource of wisdom and insight that we ignore at our peril.

In thinking of the Christian traditions, I find it helpful to make a distinction between core and periphery; that is, between, on the one hand, what is at the heart of the Christian gospel—the core—and, on the other, the multiple ways in which Christians down through the years have struggled to express and practice that gospel under changing circumstances—the periphery. The core is the central message and meaning of the faith, the gospel that remains essentially the same under changing circumstances, the *traditio*. Some might think of the core as *the* Tradition (note the upper-case *T*). The periphery includes the various ways (traditions with a lower-case *t*) that people down through the years have attempted to adapt the core to make it intelligible in their time and place: in other words, the *traditum*.

One problem with the core-periphery distinction is that "periphery" covers a lot of territory. It can signify not only relatively small traditions (congregational dress codes, for example, or the practice of an annual homecoming on the third Sunday of August) but also highly important traditions such as the Westminster Confession or Augsburg Confession, the liturgies in the *Book of Common Prayer*, Charles Wesley's hymns, or particular words such as "covenant," "justification," or "reconciliation." These examples make clear that some traditions (still lower-case *t*) are obviously much more central and important than others. These more central ones stand closer to the core and participate in it more fully, sharing in its normative authority. Yet they, like the less central traditions, are also historical, relative to particular times, places, and communities.[6] I have no easy solution to the indeterminateness or fuzziness of referring to all (lower-case) traditions as periphery. Perhaps an image of a continuum of relative closeness to the core will have to suffice. Nonetheless, what is important is to note not only their normativity— especially as they stand closer to the core—but also their historicity, their relative character. They always stand judged by the core narrative, *the* Tradition *(traditio)*, of which they are historical adaptations or expressions *(traditum)*.

As I indicated previously, Paul refers to this core narrative simply as "Jesus Christ and him crucified" or other similar statements. More fully expressed, it is a narrative about human sinfulness that has corrupted God's good creation, including the image of God in which all people have been created; it is about God's reconciling and redeeming grace that we know in the life, death, and resurrection of Jesus Christ; and it is about God the Holy Spirit's continuing work in building communities that witness to the hope of a new creation. Although this is a bare-bones way of expressing the core, it is this narrative to which the scriptures preeminently bear witness that is at the heart of our faith. Vincent of Lerins once described the core as "what has been believed everywhere, always, by everybody."[7] He would probably think my statement of the core extremely minimalist, but I believe that it is one way of saying what it is that animates the whole, what it is that is central to all that we do, and without which there is little reason for us to claim to be the church.

Beyond this core, as I have suggested, the periphery stretches rather far. There are the different traditions that we considered earlier: the beliefs and practices of the early Christian communities as they sought to witness to what the apostles had seen and heard. There are the stories of the earlier struggles of the people of Israel to be God's covenant people. As I view it, scripture is part of both the core and the periphery. The Bible reveals the core to us in a decisive way, but it also is the record of the diverse attempts, first of the people of Israel and later of the various early Christian communities, to give expression to the core. There are also the councils and creeds and confessions and various denominational distinctives, such as the Reformed or Lutheran or Anglican or Wesleyan traditions. Liturgies, hymns, and other sacred musical forms are another part of our traditions, as are also various practices that have developed over time. Let us not forget local traditions, not only dress codes and special days but congregational stories, symbols, perspectives, and practices that are highly cherished and come out of congregations' past efforts to be faithful to God's purposes. All of these represent ways that Christians, under changing circumstances, have struggled to say what it means to believe and practice in faithfulness to the God who is known in Jesus Christ.

The variety of answers reflect the ongoing process of traditioning and retraditioning. Not all are equal. We accord greater authority to some than to others, especially those that were closest to the central events of our faith, or those on which churches have reached broad ecumenical consensus, or those that have stood the test of time. But all of these are relative and provisional. They are there for us to appropriate critically and reflexively as we seek guidance from them, but not for us to give unquestioned authority. So then, what is their role for us as we try to exercise the freedom God has given us to construct innovative strategies of action in our congregations?

One role is quite pragmatic. Traditions signal boundaries that, if crossed through innovation, often precipitate conflict. Congregations and their members, no matter how progressive, have traditions—local or denominational—that are sacred to them and that they often fight to preserve. A United Church of Christ congregation in Connecticut debated for three years whether to accept the gift of a cross to be hung on the chancel wall behind the pulpit. Older members, especially, were steeped in the Congregational tradition of the plain meetinghouse. It did not seem natural to them to have a cross hanging in the meeting room, as they called the sanctuary. Likewise, "music wars" arise when someone, typically the pastor, attempts to change the style of music that the congregation sings. The new songs do not sound like hymns! Fights over inclusive language have plagued other congregations. In all these cases, traditions created boundaries that were in danger of being violated. Avoiding such conflicts is no excuse for ducking change when change is required, but neglecting or ignoring these cherished traditions is a sure way to doom efforts at change to failure.

There are, however, much more important and positive roles for the traditions side of the dialectic. Quite simply, to ignore the churches' traditions is to ignore an important means of grace. The accumulated wisdom of the church's practices as it has struggled through the years with what it means to be faithful is a rich resource for inspiration and guidance as we face our own challenges. Our traditions re-present that wisdom and make it available to us. Augustine or Luther or Calvin or Wesley cannot tell us what we are to do in our present situation. They can, however, be enlisted as consultants, as the theologian John Meagher (1990: 252) put it pithily; but, as he also reminds us, "they have no veto and can cast their votes only by cooperative proxy." Still, we can learn from them how they and other Christians sought to give expression to the Christian story as they responded to challenges that they faced and thus created traditions that have come down to us.

If we enlist them as consultants, we may also find them to be a catalyst for change as we discover aspects of the tradition that we have neglected and that, when acknowledged, challenge us to rethink our congregational practices. In an earlier book (Carroll 1991: 170ff.), I cited a simple but important example of this in the experience of a former student in a Doctor of Ministry program. The student was a pastor of a Pentecostal-Holiness congregation. In one of his courses, his imagination was captured by reading about what has been called "the Great Reversal" that occurred in the late nineteenth and early twentieth centuries: the shift of many evangelical Protestant groups, including his own, away from vigorous efforts to address social evils such as slavery to an almost exclusive focus on individual salvation. The more he read about this "forgotten" part of his Pentecostal-Holiness heritage and, in other courses, the more he immersed himself in biblical accounts of Jesus' ministry, the more he was troubled by his own and the congregation's narrow, inward focus. Consequently, in his preaching and teaching, he began to lead his congregation in reflection on what he called "faithfulness to the whole Christ." Together they studied their denomination's history; they invited speakers from social agencies to the congregation; and they began to ask, concretely, what steps they could take to witness to the "whole Christ." Out of this came small but important steps of social ministry as a way of reclaiming their tradition that had been hidden to them.

In this way traditions, sometimes even hidden or neglected traditions, are critical components of our tool kit in informing new strategies of action. Medieval theologians called these hidden elements of the tradition "shadow traditions"—things that had been dropped, neglected, or rejected but that nevertheless remained in the shadows. When recovered, they can make important contributions to shaping innovative strategies of action. While they are not exactly hidden, we might well ask today what we can learn from the Christian tradition about such things as spiritual healing, which is now being rediscovered by the medical profession, or even what has been the church's experience with angels, who suddenly have emerged (or "landed"?) in popular religious and secular culture.

Traditions, including the various denominational traditions in which we stand—Reformed, Wesleyan, or Anglican, for example—also give us a language and grammar of faith, what George Lindbeck (1984) has called a cultural-linguistic system that we use to name and interpret our experiences. Or, to use Wallace Stevens's imagery to which I referred earlier, it is our traditions, our inherited language and perspectives, that we use to construct our descriptions of our "places" and experiences. This is well illustrated by African-American Christians. From slavery onward, they have found the language and stories of the Bible, but especially Israel's stories of exodus and liberation, to be powerful aids in naming and interpreting their experiences. A similar use of tradition for naming and interpreting experience goes on in posttraditional churches. Donald Miller (1997: 72–73) interviewed members of "new paradigm" churches about their conversion. While they reported having experienced dissatisfaction with their life and lifestyle that precipitated their conversion, they were not on an intellectual quest. They did not, for example, carefully weigh various religious or philosophical traditions to determine which was superior in trying to resolve their dissatisfaction. Instead, they seized on the language and symbols of Christian conversion and rebirth, which

they, as Americans, had absorbed while growing up, to help them interpret their experience of dissatisfaction and its resolution. For them, as
with African-Americans, traditions provided language and grammar for
interpreting experience. Is it not also possible that younger generations
more generally, Boomers and Generation Xers, may find in our traditions
the means for endowing their experiences with meaning and significance?

Finally, we neglect tradition(s) in our congregational (and personal)
life at the peril of losing our Christian identity and falling victim to
whatever fads and fashions come our way, whether the fads have
integrity from the standpoint of the core tradition or not. In *After Virtue,*
Alasdair MacIntyre (1984: 221–22) reminds us that who we are is in
large part what we inherit. We inherit "a specific past that is present to
some degree in [our] present." We cannot know what we are to do, he
suggests, unless we also know the story or stories of which we are a part
(p. 216). At the same time, however, the nature of the complex, pluralistic, posttraditional world in which we live means that our traditions no
longer prescribe what we are to do to be faithful, as they might have
done in a world more attuned to tradition and its authority. New occasions do teach new duties. Nonetheless, the new duties and the new
practices that they require, including ecclesial practices, gain their
integrity as they are shaped by the spirit, not the letter, of the tradition(s)
in which we stand, especially the core, Jesus Christ and him crucified.

Testing the spirits of innovative ecclesial practices is the heart of the
questions raised for both posttraditional and more conventional mainstream churches. For mainstream churches, the question is how to honor
the tradition(s) while being open to the Spirit's leading in uncharted territory. The question for posttraditional churches is whether, in their
efforts to adapt ecclesial practices to be culturally relevant, they have
sometimes confused the spirit of the age with the Holy Spirit. As I have
tried to show in this chapter, this is not a new question. It was already
being addressed by the first Christian communities, and it has been
faced time and again throughout the church's history. But the peculiarly
unsettling character of posttraditional society makes it an exceptionally
pressing issue for today.

Paul's dialectic of tradition *and* freedom has much to commend it. I
have argued that the challenges of our particular context call for erring
on the side of freedom without ignoring the continuing role of tradition.
Remembering who and whose we are—honoring the tradition—is not
a call to live in the past. Rather, we go forward remembering. In a reflective conversation with scripture and tradition, we let those stories and
the examples of our predecessors inform our present practices without

determining them. And we exercise the freedom that we have in Christ to construct new practices for the sake of our children and our children's children. In this dual way, churches both transmit culture—our faith traditions and institutional practices—and produce culture—new practices that will become traditions for generations to come.

What more specifically this might mean for mainline churches and what we can learn from the posttraditional churches is the subject of the final chapter.

4

Raising Dry Bones: What Can We Learn From Posttraditional Congregations?

Mortal, can these bones live?

Ezekiel 37:3

I began the introduction to this book with the story from Edward Bellamy's *Looking Backward*, which depicted what Bellamy thought church life in the twentieth century would be like. He was prescient in some ways and wrong in others. In contrast to Bellamy, I have not tried to develop a picture of church life in the twenty-first century. Considering the enormous number of social and cultural changes that have profoundly affected all aspects of life in the twentieth century, including church life, it would be impossible, if not foolish, to try to anticipate all the changes that might occur over the course of the next century. Instead, I have argued that for the present we might do well to consider how detraditionalization is affecting our local ecclesial structures and practices and what it might imply in terms of openness to innovation. I have also argued that the posttraditional congregations might be considered in many respects to be bellwether institutions from which other congregations can learn—without necessarily becoming their clones— as they move into the new century.

When the prophet Ezekiel considered the plight of the Israelites in exile in Babylon, he asked, "Can these dry bones live?" This is the question being asked about many tradition-directed congregations today, which includes most of those from mainline traditions. What, then, are some of the lessons that posttraditional churches have to teach that may assist in breathing life into our ecclesial forms and practices as we seek to be Christ's body in a new century? Before attempting an answer, I begin with two cautions—reasons for not simply adapting our practices uncritically in imitation of posttraditional ecclesial styles.

Caveat Emptor

The adage appropriate to commercial transactions, caveat emptor, "let the buyer beware," is also applicable to uncritical borrowing from posttraditional congregations. So let me state my cautions and make a plea for careful discernment as we ask how we might respond to detraditionalization.

The primary caution for not buying the whole loaf of posttraditional church practices is theological. As I have argued, every congregation must judge itself by how its ecclesial life—its ministries and practices—is faithful to its calling to be Christ's body in its particular time and place. That is the core criterion for discernment. When I apply this test to some strategies and practices of posttraditional churches such as some of those described in chapter 3, I find them theologically deficient. For example, the almost overriding concern with growth, with building ever bigger congregations, borders on an idolatry of size. There is nothing intrinsically wrong with large churches, nor is there anything intrinsically worthy about being small; but if, for example, one listens to conversations among clergy and observes what gets held up and honored at denominational gatherings, it seems clear that growth has supplanted faithfulness as the test by which congregations are judged.

The practices of some posttraditional congregations also raise questions about the integrity of the congregation's witness. For example, some of the worship services I have experienced in posttraditional congregations have seemed more geared to attract and entertain an ever larger number of participants than to lead them in the adoration of God, which is the core of Christian worship. Although I was previously somewhat critical of Marva Dawn (1995) and other liturgical specialists for overreacting to the worship practices of posttraditional churches, I agree with her that some of their practices do "dumb down" the divine-human encounter that worship mediates. They have become performances for an audience of spectators rather than worshipers. The content of the music and sermons also seems at times to downplay or ignore much of what the gospel teaches about human sinfulness and brokenness or the costs of discipleship. The gospel is sometimes packaged so neatly that its hard edges are blunted or missed altogether. Many praise choruses are sloppily sentimental, individualistic, and subjective, though perhaps no more so than some of the nineteenth-century gospel hymns that have become part of the cherished tradition of many congregations.[1] Rock and grunge as musical idioms for worship jar sensibilities and to some, myself included, seem deficient for lifting one's spirit in praise of God. Popular theology, as articulated in small-group discussions, risks creating God in the group's image rather than vice versa. In his study of small spiritual growth groups, Robert Wuthnow (1994: 239) found that such groups play an important role in helping members to experience God as real in the nitty-gritty of everyday life. But, he notes, participants also sometimes make God into a good buddy, on the same level with themselves, one whom they can reach out and touch. In doing so they risk losing any sense of God's otherness and transcendence, which sometimes have led believers—even Jesus himself—to experience God as hidden or silent.

Similar criticisms can be directed at efforts to detraditionalize church architecture by making it look no different from the spaces in which we live in the secular worlds of work, family, and leisure. Are we not to some extent impoverished when we substitute converted warehouses or buildings devoid of any religious symbols for spaces that speak to us of God's transcendence or God's immanence? Is this not to ignore the important contribution that well-designed, theologically sensitive church architecture can make to Christian formation?

When such theological objections to their practices are offered, posttraditional church leaders often counter with their own theological rationale: It is true, they say, that they want to grow; they do want to attract new members, but church growth is not for the sake of growth alone. Rather they are following Jesus' command to make disciples so that those who come as seekers might be formed into fully devoted followers of Christ. If this goal is to be achieved in today's world, these leaders say, it will not be through the use of traditional methods. If worship practices turn off and turn away the "Unchurched Harrys and Marys" who come as seekers, if they appear boring and irrelevant to a generation raised on MTV, then how will they ever hear the gospel? If traditional hymns, pipe organs, sermons, programs, and church architecture are alien not only to seekers but to members, they will not stay. Nontraditional and unconventional strategies are required.

Although it is true that the attraction of growth and ever bigger congregations sometimes appears to override all other justifications and risks idolatry, this kind of pragmatic theology of posttraditional leaders is not without merit. In their ecclesial strategies are echoes of Jesus' use of familiar, ordinary, everyday events and experiences to convey his quite extraordinary gospel; and there are his warnings about placing stumbling blocks in the path of little ones to hinder their believing (Matthew 18:6). Posttraditional leaders also cite Paul's example: "I have become all things to all people, that I might by all means save some" (1 Corinthians 9:22).

Still, there are clear dangers to an uncritical pragmatism, dangers faced by Jesus in his time of testing in the wilderness. There the tempter called on Jesus to turn stones to bread, to make a dramatic statement by throwing himself from a tower, and to bow down to the devil—all with the "good" end of winning the masses to his cause (Matthew 4:1–11). But Jesus' refusal of this promised "good" in the name of his unwavering obedience to God alone is a decisive moment in his ministry, and it is a key to understanding the gospel story. His temptation experience is not only a statement about how we as individual Christians are to practice faithfulness, but it is especially a word to the church about the costs of discipleship, about the need to test our ecclesial life and practices by Jesus' story. This means learning when to say no and when to say yes. There are clearly no easy answers to this dilemma. The choices that confront us are part and parcel of the freedom that we have in Christ. Yet, as I have indicated, I find some posttraditional church practices wanting—exhibiting too uncritical a compromise with the tempter who promises that seekers will fill our pews to overflowing and that large size and spectacular programs will attract even more.

When I am honest with myself, however, I realize that it is not only a difference in theological perspective that leads to some of my objections made under the guise of theology. I suspect that some are really a reflection of the generation of which I am a part, and others are simply matters of taste. Generational differences in preferred congregational styles are pronounced. What attracts Baby Boomers may have little appeal to Generation Xers. An even bigger divide in preferences exists between those who, like me, were born prior to World War II, and those born since 1945. The experiences of our formative years were considerably different from those of Boomers and Xers, and these experiences have a decisive but often unrecognized impact on our preferences in many areas of life, including ecclesial practices.

Furthermore, matters of taste, not all of which are generational, also enter in. Some of the sharp critiques of posttraditional church liturgical and music styles may say more about the cultural tastes of the critics—myself included—than our theological acuity. Theologian Richard Mouw has argued this point in a short book, *Consulting the Faithful* (1994). He defends what some view as the "tacky theology" of popular religious expressions against attacks by religious elites, arguing that the latter have often based their criticisms as much on matters of taste as on theological criteria. Mouw's is an important warning to those of us who dismiss posttraditional practices: Are we doing so primarily for valid theological reasons, or are we doing so on matters of taste or because our generational sensibilities are offended?

A second reason that existing congregations should exercise caution in adapting the strategies of action of posttraditional congregations is the simple fact that many existing congregations could not do so even if they wanted to. Some of the strategies would clearly not fit. Many of the posttraditional churches that we hold up as exemplars are new congregations, and in some cases they have no denominational relationship. Their leaders started them from scratch and they were relatively unconstrained by any traditions, denominational or otherwise. In contrast, existing congregations not only have their denominational heritage to which they owe some degree of allegiance, but they also already have their own local traditions, their own stories and practices; they have some material and human resources and not others; and they exist in particular social and cultural contexts. All of this affects the capacity of existing congregations to change. Congregations may desperately need to change, to adopt new strategies of action, but saying so and doing so are two quite different enterprises. The old adage that "you can't make a silk purse out of a sow's ear" is at least partially true when it comes to congregations as well as individuals. Who we are and where we are as congregations set limits on what we can become—at least in the short run.

I have been involved for a number of years in what has come to be called congregational studies. If we have learned anything in our work, it is that congregations are complex systems that do not readily yield either to easy understanding or quick-fix efforts to change. Yet we have also learned that congregations can change. Sows' ears can become silk purses, but each silk purse will have its own character. And the character that emerges will reflect what the congregation brings to the change effort out of its past and present, including its particular take or perspective on the Christian tradition, and the specific demands and challenges of its social and cultural context.

Some Lessons from Posttraditional Congregations

With these qualifications against an uncritical adoption of the practices of posttraditional congregations, let me come back to the question with which I began. What can more traditional congregations learn from these churches as they move into the new millennium? I will deal with five lessons, each of which could be the subject of a much longer treatment.

Erring on the Side of Freedom: Reflexive Ecclesiology

The primary lesson is one that can be made briefly since it reiterates my argument of the previous chapter. I believe that mainline churches, following the lead of posttraditional churches, should be bold in exercising the freedom that we are given in Jesus Christ to develop ecclesial practices that are both faithful to the gospel *and* appropriate to the social and cultural challenges of posttraditional society. If we must choose between following well-worn, customary, and cherished paths of church practice, however faithful they are to the gospel narrative, and embracing culturally sensitive innovations that also appear to have gospel integrity, then let our choice be on the side of freedom. To do this requires breaking the "but-we've-always-done-it-this-way" mentality that infects both members and leaders alike, not only about beloved local traditions but also about those that have come down to us from the history of the church—music, worship styles, organizational practices, and so forth. It means refusing slavish adherence to these traditions in favor of a process of reflective discernment in which we examine our cherished practices in the light of posttraditional realities. Such discernment involves seeking the guidance of the Holy Spirit as we adapt old ways and shape new practices, new ways of "being church," some of which are suggested by the ecclesiologies of the new-style churches. To do so is to practice a kind of reflexivity when it comes to ecclesiology, acknowledging the "event" or movement character of the church in contrast to being overly concerned with its institutional or tradition-directed character.

Yet, as I have also tried to make clear, I do not advocate simply jettisoning the church's traditions (small *t*) willy-nilly as do some enthusiasts for posttraditional churches. Many of our traditions are important means of grace that we ignore at our peril. They embody a collective memory and wisdom without which we would be impoverished. Many traditional practices continue to be important means for spiritual growth. What is called for is the selective retrieval of those aspects of our traditions that were forged in previous times and places as Christians attempted to be faithful to the gospel, and that, appropriately adapted, may help us today in our search for fidelity. Such traditions—creeds, liturgies, hymns, gestures, and practices—can be reflexively drawn on and retraditionalized in ways that keep them living rather than dead.

To reiterate, selective retrieval and adaptation of traditions imply a stance toward tradition that is far different from that of earlier times, when few would dare question the tradition's authority. Yet the characteristics of posttraditional society make such a stance imperative. The locus of authority has shifted from the tradition itself to the individual—from "out there" to "in here"—making it imperative that we exercise our freedom to choose those traditions that will guide us individually or as communities.

Strong, Shared Leadership

A second lesson that posttraditional churches teach is the critical importance of leadership. In one sense, to say that leadership is the sine qua non for developing innovative and effective organizations is so commonplace that it seems hardly worth mentioning. Shelves are full of books on leadership, some helpful, some not. But this attention to the importance of leadership is indicative of the posttraditional world in which we live. We are not at all sure that the past is a reliable guide for the future, or that our traditional institutional forms, ecclesial or otherwise, are adequate to the challenge. Well-worn paths supplied by traditions do not always lead where we need or desire to go. So we look to leadership that can help us find our way in uncharted territory—leadership that practices reflexivity in ecclesiological matters.

When one looks at new-style churches in particular, one of the qualities that genuinely stands out in many of them is innovative, entrepreneurial leadership that often exhibits reflexivity. Recall the comment of management guru Peter Drucker that these congregations are "the only social institution [in America] that is healthy and growing." Drucker attributes their health to the quality of their leadership.

What, especially, seems characteristic of posttraditional church leaders? At best, they are leaders who have been able to discern a need by listening to folks inside and outside the church express their spiritual yearnings; who have been able to imagine new ways of responding to those needs that they believe are consistent with the gospel; and who have been able to coalesce others around that vision, mobilize the congregation's resources, and help the congregation embody the vision in congregational practices. As I have said, one may not agree with everything that these leaders do or with all aspects of their leadership, but they model a style of leadership from which other congregational leaders can learn.

Sometimes the vision is that of a particular person, a pastor for example, such as in the case of Chapel Hill Bible Church, a congregation that I mentioned in chapter 3. The congregation emerged from the vision some twenty-five years ago of Jim Abrahamson, who continues to serve as its teaching pastor. Abrahamson saw a need for a biblically based congregation that would serve as an evangelical Christian witness in a university community. Giving congregational flesh to the vision meant combining those three elements—biblically based, evangelical, and university setting—and developing strategies of action that would embody that vision. Abrahamson did not do it alone. He brought together a team of "elders," some ordained but mostly lay, who shared or caught his vision and helped to bring it into being.

At other times the initial vision is that of a group of laity who realize that their congregation must change if it is to survive in the face of some new challenge and who are willing to go through the struggle and conflict necessary to bring it into being. In the mid-1970s, First Presbyterian Church in Jamaica, Queens, found itself in the midst of a racially and ethnically changing neighborhood that had resulted in the loss of many white members to the suburbs. They knew that if their congregation was to survive, they would have to reach out to the new people moving in. With the help of an interim minister, a group of lay leaders decided that their future lay in becoming a multiracial, multicultural congregation. They actively sought a pastor who shared that vision and brought the necessary expertise to lead them toward its realization. The new pastor walked the streets asking people what they knew about the church and how they felt about their community. With this information, he and the lay leaders began to identify the gap between their vision and the reality of the congregation's current life. Together they agreed on a design for a multicultural congregation. Now, over twenty years and a second pastor later, that vision is a reality (Stark 1993: 99–108).

Both of these congregations are large in comparison to the majority of Protestant churches. In contrast, Hillsborough (N.C.) United Methodist Church is a midsized congregation founded over two hundred years ago with some five hundred members at present. What is unusual about the congregation, for Methodists in particular, is the tenure of its minister, the Reverend Herman Ward, who has served as the church's pastor for almost thirty years. Partly because of his long tenure, but especially because of the mutual trust that has developed between him and his parishioners over the years of his service, he has been able to permit and encourage the development of innovative ministries, some of which are adapted from posttraditional congregations. For example, he and his lay leaders have recently developed a program to encourage members to identify and use their gifts for ministry. The program, which has been enthusiastically received in the congregation, had its impetus among several lay members who read of a similar program in a large, posttraditional United Methodist congregation in Alabama. With Ward's encouragement and support, they

visited the Alabama church, learned about its program, and adapted it to
fit their considerably smaller congregation. His is an established congregation that has been able to incorporate some of the practices of new-style
churches into its life—and a key part of the reason that this has happened
has been Ward's leadership style, based on mutual trust between the
leader and the congregation.[2]

Leadership that can bring off such innovation, as in these three examples, is not an easy task. It does not mean simply copying what someone
else has done. Rather it involves envisioning, preferably shared broadly
with laity, what a congregation might become, and then seeing the connections between present reality and the vision for the future.

The contrasts among the examples are also instructive. In the case of
Chapel Hill Bible Church (and of many other posttraditional congregations, including Willow Creek), the leader was starting de novo to build
a congregation, and, in this case, one not affiliated with a denomination.
Because of this, Abrahamson and others who assisted in the church's
founding were to a large extent free to innovate and were unbound by
denominational or congregational traditions.[3] In the second and third
examples, pastors and laity were in part at least constrained by what
their congregations already were—their existing members, their local
traditions and culture, and their Presbyterian and Methodist denominational affiliations.

While traditions such as these can be important resources as leaders
try to envision and build a new future, they also can be constraints and
sometimes even hindrances. In such cases, circumstances may require
challenging existing traditions and the often unspoken guiding assumptions that members hold about what their congregation should be or do.
Without such challenges, members may not be able to see beyond what
currently exists and imagine new possibilities for their corporate life
that are faithful to God's purposes for them in this time and place.

In Samuel Freedman's intriguing book about St. Paul Community
Baptist Church in Brooklyn, Freedman describes how the Reverend
Johnny Ray Youngblood led St. Paul through a process of transformation from a moribund, dying congregation in a depressed and crime-
infested inner-city community to a vibrant and vital congregation—a
"Church Unusual" as they now describe themselves in their mission
statement. The situation was so bad when Youngblood accepted the call
to St. Paul that a fellow pastor called the church "one of God's Alca-
trazes." As Freedman (1993: 96) writes:

> Reverend Youngblood [found himself] at war with tradition—
> if not with the proud history of the black church, then certainly

with the customs passed unquestioningly from generation to generation. He announced the battle in myriad ways—reading the Emancipation Proclamation from the pulpit, telling critics he shed "two tears in a bucket" for their concerns, and most of all repeating one favorite parable. A little girl sees her mother cutting the wings off a chicken she is about to roast. When the little girl asks why, the mother says, "Because that's the way my momma always did it." So the girl asks her grandmother, who answers, "Because that's the way *my* momma always did it." Finally the girl asks her great-grandmother, who says, "Because my pan was too small."

Finally leaders must work with the congregation to develop resources, programs, and practices that embody that vision in their common life. In short, the vision must be institutionalized. It does little good to challenge traditions or envision new possibilities unless one can move toward the vision with appropriate programs and practices. How is this accomplished? My own and others' research on posttraditional congregations has highlighted the important way in which leaders in these congregations exercise authority. They are not shrinking violets, nor are they laissez-faire enablers. But *neither are they authoritarian despots who must control every aspect of the congregation's life!* I emphasize this point because it is easy to ignore what may be one of the most distinctive aspects of the leadership of many of these pastors and a key to their effectiveness.[4] While some (not all) may be the primary "announcers of the congregation's vision," they permit, encourage, and empower others—other staff and lay members—to develop programs and practices that embody the vision in a variety of ways in the congregation's life, as was the case, for example, in the Hillsborough congregation.

In his study of Vineyard, Calvary Chapel, and Hope Chapel congregations, the sociologist Donald Miller (1997: 138) describes leadership practices in these three movements as follows: "The senior pastor sets the vision and defines the spiritual culture of the institution, but he typically gives substantial autonomy to individual staff members in overseeing specific programs. There is a strong sentiment that the real work of ministry is done by the people, so the clergy see their task as nurturing and training lay leaders rather than initiating programs and running them." Miller continues: "Leaders create a 'corporate' culture in which excellence is expected, and yet, they give relative autonomy to their staff and members in implementing the vision they so skillfully articulate. From inside the organization, things may appear a little messy—because people are grabbing hold of the vision at many different levels—but

hierarchical boundaries are not important so long as the job is getting
done" (p. 140).

Leaders of these congregations establish their authority or right to
lead not primarily by virtue of the office they hold or because of their formal credentials, but more by a combination of demonstrated competence
and religious authenticity. They are perceived as having their "head and
heart" together. Theirs is a personal authority that creates what Ronald
Heifetz, in *Leadership Without Easy Answers* (1994), has called "a holding environment." A holding environment is a relationship in which a
leader's personal or informal authority gives the leader the power to hold
the attention of others and help them to do the necessary adaptive work
to face some particular challenge. For example, Heifetz described how
an oncologist's relationship with her patients helped create a holding
environment that enabled a family to face and prepare for the husband's
approaching death from cancer. She gave them the resources and support
they needed to do the work they had to do. That is not unlike Miller's
description of what the leaders of posttraditional churches do. Put in
Heifetz's terms, these pastors use their authority not only to articulate a
vision for the congregation's ministry but also to create a holding environment where they give the work of the ministry back to the people. As
Miller says of the pastors in these congregations: "many . . . are very
strong visionaries. . . . [They] maintain veto power over programs. But
their primary role is to inspire, lend confidence, and work on the spiritual development of the individual" (p. 139). For Herman Ward, the pastor of the midsized United Methodist congregation, the holding
environment that he has established is the fruit of his long tenure and
effective pastoral care of several generations of church members.

These examples illustrate that exercising leadership in the holding
environment is not only inspirational but also at heart educative. While
in the case of the posttraditional congregations, the focus is primarily
on individual growth—making fully committed disciples—such leadership builds congregational capacities as well. The congregation itself
becomes a learning community, as in the example of Ward's Hillsborough congregation. In their work together around a shared vision, both
members and leaders gain new capacities for facing the changing
demands of ministry in unsettled times.

Although I have only touched on the major characteristics of the
model of leadership that is characteristic of many posttraditional congregations, I want to highlight its importance even more sharply by
describing a contrasting style. In research on congregations in changing
communities, sociologist Nancy Ammerman (1997a: 326–27) found

that pastoral leadership was one of the key reasons that congregations either adapted creatively to change or failed to do so. In adapting congregations pastors tended to exhibit many leadership capacities similar to those in posttraditional congregations. In contrast, in congregations that hunkered down in the face of change and sought to maintain the status quo, Ammerman found that "Pastors . . . tended not to introduce new ideas and programs. Most provided excellent care of the people in their congregations and performed well the duties expected of them. Most fit nicely with their parishioners, working hard to maintain the pattern of church life all of them expected. If they perceived any need for change, they were often unwilling or unable to undertake the difficult (and often conflictual) work of dislodging old routines. A few expressed . . . their sense that their leadership skills were simply not up to the challenges they knew the congregation faced. Others simply pastored the best they knew how" (1997a: 327).

The question is, why the difference? Is the capacity to exercise leadership a spiritual gift that not everyone has, as some have suggested,[5] or can it be learned? It may be that some who become ordained ministers simply do not have the gift to exercise leadership, whether such capacity is a gift of the Spirit or a more natural potential that can be nurtured and developed. If so, perhaps they should be helped to find other ways to exercise their calling to ministry than as leaders of congregations, or, alternatively, learn to identify and nurture laity within their congregations who can exercise the needed leadership. On the other hand, could it be that at least some of the pastors of the kind that Ammerman described have the potential for exercising leadership, but this potential has not been nurtured and developed? There is no way to give a definitive answer to these important questions, but they deserve the serious attention of all who are concerned with recruiting, educating, and supporting clergy and lay leadership for the church of the twenty-first century. If we can learn anything from the posttraditional congregations, it is the crucial importance of having innovative leaders who are not afraid to forge new ecclesial paths in uncharted territory.

Hard Eggs or Spanish Inns?

A third lesson from posttraditional congregations has to do with their focus on the needs of members or potential members, often using needs-assessment strategies drawn from market research. Let me address this strategy and those who have criticized it with a story.

When I sat for the French reading exam for the Ph.D. degree, I was handed an article to translate from a French theological journal. I looked at the title and had difficulty believing what I thought it said. The title was "The Spanish Inn or the Hard Egg." Could that be right? If so, what might it mean, and what did it have to do with theology? As I read on, I discovered that I had indeed translated the title correctly. The article was built around two stories: one about a Spanish inn where, if you knew how to ask for it, you could get anything you wanted; the other was about a monastery whose abbot forced each member of the community to swallow a hard egg every morning. The two stories were used to characterize two theological approaches: The Spanish inn represented Friedrich Schleiermacher's theological method. The hard egg story was used to characterize Karl Barth's approach. The author advocated neither and instead extolled Rudolf Bultmann as offering a more adequate method. But it is not to argue about theological method that I recount the story; rather my aim is to contrast two approaches to congregational life and practices.

Many of the posttraditional churches would appear to be Spanish inns as they assess the needs of their target audience and then shape their programs to meet those needs. Believing that many potential members find traditional worship spaces and worship practices off-putting, these congregations create nontraditional spaces and eliminate Christian symbols in order not to turn off those that they are trying to reach. They substitute soft and sometimes hard rock and praise choruses for many of the traditional hymns of the church. They also develop small-group opportunities that address the needs that their surveys have identified. In short, they function like the proverbial Spanish inn.

Some of the sharpest criticisms of the new-style churches, including my own earlier in this chapter, have been aimed at them for this Spanish inn approach, where people are given what they want if they know how to ask for it. These criticisms are in some respects justified, as I noted. The gospel is not always "seeker friendly." It is not simply about feeling good, or being entertained, or having our itches scratched, to put it somewhat inelegantly. It is not a road to prosperity, as is the not-so-subtle message of some of the new-style churches. Furthermore, I dislike the language of marketing one's congregation, although admittedly we have frequently done so under other names.

So is the hard egg strategy more appropriate? It depends on what hard egg we mean. If it means confronting people with "the whole Christ," as my former student put it (see chapter 3), then yes, the hard egg approach is appropriate. If it means that God calls us to drink the cup of obedience, which is not always a cup of good cheer, then yes again for the hard egg strategy. If, as I emphasized above, it means being honest with people about the costs of discipleship, then yes once more. If, in short, the hard egg approach means being engaged by the church's core Tradition (capital *T*)—Jesus Christ and him crucified—then this approach is appropriate.

On the other hand, if the hard egg approach means being inattentive to people's needs, then no. If it means being dismissive of popular forms of religious piety and practice just because they seem tacky to us, then no again. If it means that those of us who are professional theologians, or liturgists, or musicians, or pastors always know better than the people in the pews, then no once again, doubly so.

When we consult Jesus' ministry and teachings we get a picture of an interesting strategy that is neither hard egg nor Spanish inn. We can readily point to his hard sayings that challenge us to a costly discipleship and to his demonstration of that costliness in his obedience unto death. We dare not play these down in the interest of congregational growth. But we must also be attentive to the ways that Jesus used common, everyday experiences and metaphors in his teaching, and the way that he addressed people in terms of the particularities of their contexts and needs. This is evident in the stories of healing or feeding or personal transformation where Jesus made good on the promises of his inaugural sermon in Nazareth. In short, Jesus made God present to the people whom he encountered in words and actions that they could clearly understand, in ways that were context- and need-sensitive. That, as I understand it, is one of the clear meanings of the incarnation—that the Word became flesh and tabernacled (literally "pitched tent") among us so that we could encounter the mystery of God in the midst of this rough-and-tumble world. John Calvin described God's pedagogy with this interesting analogy: "as nurses commonly do with infants, God is wont in a measure to 'lisp' in speaking to us."[6]

If we accept the incarnational principle, then we may be much more open to expressions of faith and practice that, from a high aesthetic, would be considered tacky or lowbrow but that speak to the needs and experiences of people in the congregation. We may also be better able to appreciate these words of John Wimber, the founder of the Vineyard Movement: "As a young church, we experience all of the opportunities and problems which accompany youth. Our young 18-to-25-year-old attenders are providing the spiritual dynamic which enables us to reach out to a young culture and relate the Gospel to them. Because we are young, we are current. We speak the language of these people. Our sermons and songs are familiar and acceptable. We find ourselves communicating eternal truths in a contemporary style."[7] Wimber's words echo the comment of the pastor of the posttraditional church cited in chapter 2 who said that they give people what they want, while at the same time they "give them what they didn't know they wanted." This strategy is not too different from that which we encounter in Jesus' ministry. With appropriate cautions, it is not a bad strategy for those of us in mainline churches.

Let me draw several important inferences from this perspective that I will simply state without much elaboration. First, it argues strongly for an interactive rather than elitist approach to ministry in the congregation. It argues for a style in which clergy and other professional staff refuse to assume that they always know best and that the concerns, feelings, and tastes of lay members are unimportant. Lay members, as well as those who are outside the congregation, may not always be able to articulate their deepest insights, yearnings, and experiences of God in ways that would pass muster in Systematic Theology 101. Yet laity inside and outside the church often exhibit substantial practical theological wisdom that should be listened to, learned from, and built upon rather than ignored.[8] This is a special challenge for those of us who teach, preach, choose, or lead music for worship, revise hymnals[9] and books of worship, or develop program materials for use in local congregations.[10] Accepting popular religious expressions as indicative of deep spiritual yearnings, clergy and other religious professionals can use these yearnings as starting points for nurturing deeper faith.

Second, generational, class, and ethnic differences play important roles in influencing how people hear, understand, and interpret the gospel; how they worship; what hymns and music they appreciate; and what needs they bring to congregational involvement. Many of us know this in principle but ignore it in practice. Knowing one's congregation, knowing how similar or different members and prospective members are in lifestyles and needs, and finding ways of honoring and respecting this diversity are crucial for both current and future ecclesial forms and practices.[11] The ability of posttraditional churches to be culturally current, to speak in the languages of the Baby Boom and Baby Bust generations, may be the most distinctive difference between them and more traditional congregations, and it also may be one of the more important lessons traditional congregations have to learn from them.

Openness to diverse cultural styles is not, however, a call to adulterate the gospel to make it palatable. To reiterate what I said above, I am not proposing a least common denominator or Spanish inn strategy. Whatever we do must not only be judged by how well it speaks the languages of the multiple cultures in our congregations, but also by its fidelity to the core story that is at the heart of our faith. There are hard edges to the gospel; there are costs of discipleship that cannot be downplayed or avoided; and they often challenge popular religious perspectives and piety. There is also a sense of the ineffable, of mystery, of the holy, that is in danger of being flattened out and lost in the blurring of sacred and secular architectural styles, music, and other cultural forms.

In chapter 2, I mentioned the group of California evangelical Baby Boomers who formed a congregation affiliated with the Antiochian Orthodox Church. As I suggested, they did so out of a need to reconnect with the historic traditions of the ancient church and the mystery and majesty that its liturgy offers. At the same time, however, they have retained many aspects of their evangelical style and commitment in an interesting mix of symbolic codes characteristic of posttraditional society. Similarly, the immense popularity, especially among youth, of worship practices adapted from the Taizé Community in France is another example of how elements of traditional spiritual practices—chants and singing—are expressed in modern garb, with considerable effectiveness. Like praise choruses, they are often based on a simple phrase repeated again and again; but unlike some praise choruses, they are more introspective and meditative.[12] Participants are encouraged to continue singing them "in their hearts" as they go about their daily work. Both illustrate reflective attempts to overcome the tension between tradition and the freedom that we have in Christ to express the gospel in new wineskins.

We must constantly remind ourselves that the gospel is not captive to any one cultural style, any particular aesthetic, any particular generational grid, social class, or ethnic group. At the same time, however, the gospel comes alive for particular people most frequently when it is expressed in the particular idiom of their culture.

Embodying the Vision: Small Groups As an Example

Earlier, I indicated that an important task of leadership is not only to nurture a vision but to institutionalize or embody it in practices that give it concrete expression. Several of the ecclesial practices of posttraditional churches could be singled out as having lessons for congregations more generally: for example, contemporary, often highly expressive, worship styles and music; the use of drama and video clips as part of worship; the downplaying of traditional church architecture and Christian symbols; the emphasis on members' claiming and exercising their spiritual gifts; or small-group ministry. Each of these is not only an attempt to embody the congregation's particular vision for ministry, but also an effort to do so in such a way that it responds to the needs of target audiences. Although mainstream churches have much to learn—positively and negatively—from several of these innovative strategies, I focus here on one that I believe is especially applicable: the effective use of small groups.

As I have noted previously, there has been a virtual explosion of small groups in recent years, especially those that are religiously inspired or religiously sponsored. The posttraditional churches have recognized the importance of small groups and have built a significant portion of their ministries around them.

It is not the case that more traditional congregations have failed to recognize the importance of small groups, or that they are new to our experience. For example, Methodism was founded with the class meeting, a disciplined small-group experience, as its basic organizational unit. Sunday school classes also have often functioned as small groups of a certain sort, although they often become routinized and inflexible in their practices. Those of us who remember the late 1950s and early 1960s will recall the enthusiasm generated by the small-group movement at that time, but which turned out to be somewhat short-lived. While there are obvious connections and continuities between these past small-group ventures and what is happening today, there is a difference, if only in the number and diversity of small groups and, most especially, in the numbers of people who turn to them for help, support, and spiritual growth. There are, I suspect, good reasons why small groups have become so widespread and popular and why posttraditional congregations have employed them as a major means of ministry.

From the side of individuals, such groups provide a way of coping with various detraditionalizing processes, processes that challenge the authority of traditional beliefs, practices, and institutions. Greater educational opportunities, increased ease of travel, job mobility, instant global communication, and greater exposure to pluralism—all of these detraditionalize us. Although such experiences are sometimes exciting and enriching, they also undermine our stable, ascribed identities; they take us away from the families and neighborhoods and communities in which we were raised; they put stress on interpersonal relationships, marriages often being a primary victim; they present us with choices that were unimaginable to our great-grandparents. They also often lead to questioning inherited religious beliefs and commitments. So we wonder if there is any coherence beyond the fragmented, disjointed lives that many of us lead. Are there religious traditions with which we can choose to identify that do offer meaning and stability? Are there others who can help us in this search?

Our society offers few institutional settings in which we can deal with such issues; few places where we can be open and honest about our feelings and yearnings with others who will be supportive and non-judgmental; few places where we can frankly discuss our religious experiences, beliefs, and doubts. If anything, such honesty, openness, and sharing are discouraged. Small groups, however, do give us a place to voice our private thoughts, beliefs, experiences, and hopes in the con-text of a supportive fellowship. Because there are many different kinds of small groups, we can pick among a variety of options depending on what we need at a particular time—like shops in a mall. They also offer community that is not tied to a definite place—like a tent rather than a fixed temple, like movements rather than institutions. They do not typ-ically require long-term commitments—an hour or two a week, and one can extricate oneself with comparative ease. All of these are qualities that are valued in a posttraditional world.

Thus it is not surprising that small groups have exploded in recent years; nor is it surprising that churches, traditional and posttraditional, have made small-group ministries an important part of their ministry strategies. The posttraditional congregations have been especially effec-tive in their small-group ministries. They have quite intentionally devel-oped a "cafeteria" of groups to serve the diverse needs of potential constituents, and they have worked at linking participation in these groups with the ministry of the larger congregation. Different types of small groups are offered as part of a conscious strategy for moving peo-ple from the periphery to the core. They are initially evangelistic tools, entry points for seekers who may be exploring, looking for short-term, nonbinding ways of becoming involved. Groups also become strategies for pastoral care, like the various forms of twelve-step recovery groups and support groups for people experiencing various life crises. Most important, they are tools for what evangelicals call "discipling"; that is, they are communities where serious Bible study, prayer, and spiritual growth can take place.[13]

I may be mistaken, but I have a clear sense that in many posttradi-tional churches, and in evangelical congregations generally, the use of small groups is much more intentional as a strategy of ministry than for those of us in traditional, mainstream congregations. We have too often seen them as "add-ons" to traditional Sunday school classes rather than something integral to the congregation's practices of education and of nourishing the spiritual life. Furthermore, we have not always been comfortable with the kind of openness, vulnerability, and sharing of deep, intimate spiritual experiences that small groups can encourage.

The author of a case study of a long-standing Bible study group in a northeastern, mainstream Presbyterian congregation described what she called a "culture of privacy" operative in the group: "a discernible pattern of prohibition against openness about personal spirituality" (Davie 1995: 135). In individual interviews with the author, the women shared a number of profound spiritual experiences but were loathe to do so in the group because of the culture of privacy that was operative in the congregation. If this culture of privacy is not simply unique to this particular congregation but part of a more general Presbyterian culture, as the author suggests, from whence does it come? Is it from Calvin's distrust of introspection and spiritual exercises, as some have maintained?[14] Perhaps, but I suspect that it also indicates a reluctance felt by members of mainline Protestant churches generally to open themselves up to others in intimate sharing of faith and doubts. Many mainline Protestants are what Dean Hoge, Benton Johnson, and Donald Luidens call "lay liberals" in their study of Presbyterian Baby Boomers (Hoge et al. 1994: 138ff.). Lay liberals are not always sure what they believe, so they would rather keep silent than make themselves vulnerable through open sharing and self-disclosure, even in a small group of trusted associates.

There are, however, positive signs that mainline churches are breaking through this culture of privacy and learning to combine disciplined study of the Bible in small groups with faith sharing, prayer, and mutual accountability. Among United Methodists, a growing number of congregations are organizing Covenant Discipleship Groups, patterned after John Wesley's class meetings, and disciplined programs of Bible study for small groups. The Kerygma series of the Presbyterian Church (U.S.A.) and the United Methodist Disciple Bible Study have been enormously successful in fostering growth in knowledge of the biblical tradition and in understanding its connection with everyday life.[15] Small groups like these are not ends in themselves, but many mainline congregations, like posttraditional churches, are discovering that they are important practices—means of grace for nurturing fully committed disciples of Christ.

Strictness or Seriousness?

The final lesson to which I call attention is more difficult to characterize. It has to do with the ethos or distinguishing character of these churches. What is it, in the last analysis, that makes these churches attractive and appealing? Besides their leadership, cultural sensitivity, and use of innovative practices such as small groups or contemporary worship, what draws people to them? There are several dimensions to an answer, not all of which are present in every new-style congregation and not all of which mainstream churches can emulate.

Some have argued that their appeal has to do with their "social strength" or "strictness." When Dean Kelley (1972) tried to explain why conservative churches were growing and liberal churches were declining, he noted that strong churches, including theologically conservative churches, have strict membership standards and make belief and behavioral demands on their members. These demanding standards, he argued, generate high commitment, discipline, and missionary zeal. They contrast sharply with the less demanding, tolerant stance of liberal churches that produces lukewarmness, individualism, and a reticence to share one's faith. Kelley wondered if churches could also be strong—generating an ardor that "catches up [member's] lives in a surge of significance and purpose" (56)—without being "strict," in the sense of being absolutist in a fundamentalistic, separatist sense.

In recent years a number of sociologists of religion have taken up Kelley's strictness thesis and revised and extended it.[16] With Kelley, they note that strict churches are willing to state clear doctrinal positions (especially belief in the absolute authority of the Bible) and behavioral expectations for members. Because the cost of membership is high, the number of "free riders"—those who enjoy the benefits of membership without paying for them—is reduced. Thus, they argue, membership is more valuable to participants than it would be in less demanding, more tolerant churches, where some take it seriously and others do not.

Is strictness the secret of the appeal of posttraditional churches? It is certainly part of the picture, especially for some of the churches that are unabashedly conservative, even fundamentalist, in their orientation. Yet the appeal of fundamentalist congregations is relatively limited, and most posttraditional churches are not separatist as classic fundamentalists are; rather, as I have emphasized, they have leaned toward the Spanish inn strategy of cultural sensitivity in order to be seeker friendly. It is true that they are more likely to be theologically conservative, and that they have certain central doctrines and moral teachings ("majors" as they are often described) that they espouse without equivocation. Those that disagree with them either do not join or, if they do join, are likely to find staying to be uncomfortable and leave. Yet there are also "minors"—doctrines and lifestyle issues that are considered less central than the majors and that permit substantial latitude in interpretation.

This combination recalls Donald Miller's observation that leaders of the posttraditional congregations he studied do not place a high premium on purity of theological doctrine. Even in biblical interpretation, there is considerable room for exploring various individual interpretations— as long as one subscribes to the Bible's primary authority. This represents a kind of bounded subjectivity. A center of objective authority sets limits on what is permissible, but within those limits, considerable individual exploration and interpretation are permitted and encouraged. In short, bounded subjectivity allows majoring in the majors and minoring in the minors.

This modified version of strictness is some distance from one that cultivates intolerance, absolutism, authoritarianism, and separation from the culture. It does, however, convey a seriousness about Christian beliefs and practices that establishes theological and lifestyle boundaries between Christians and the broader culture.[17]

Seriousness is expressed in another way by posttraditional congregations: a commitment to excellence, to doing things well as a means of honoring God. In part many large posttraditional congregations are able to offer quality ministries because their size provides a large talent pool from which to draw, greater financial resources, and the possibility of employing professionally trained staff. These several resources are simply not available to a large majority of Protestant congregations, mainline or evangelical, that are quite small in membership size and have limited financial resources. Doing things well, however, needs to be contextually defined. What, for example, might excellence mean for a congregation that averages seventy-five in weekly attendance in contrast to Willow Creek's fifteen thousand? Clearly it does not mean offering a broad range of professionally produced programs with state-of-the-art facilities and equipment; nor does it necessarily mean having professionally trained leadership. Rather, excellence for such a congregation means a commitment to using the available resources— the gifts of the leaders and members, buildings, money, and other material resources—to their fullest capacity. It means not being satisfied with halfhearted, carelessly presented worship services and programs. One of Jesus' parables (Matthew 25:14–30) reminds us that whether one has one talent or five, what is crucial is a willingness to invest ones' resources faithfully. Doing things well, honoring God with a commitment to excellence in one's congregational life, is an important way of investing one's resources faithfully and seriously, regardless of the size of the return on one's investment.

Finally, in trying to understand the appeal of posttraditional congregations, it is important to note that seriousness for them by no means implies a somber, dour ecclesial style. Posttraditional congregations typically exhibit a spirit or élan that, they believe, contrasts sharply with the tameness, blandness, and predictability of traditional congregational life. What they believe they are doing is modeling the New Testament church of the book of Acts, which was Spirit-led and thus "fresh and energetic and creative and dynamic and unpredictable" (Hybels and Hybels 1995: 47). In some cases, especially those that have borrowed from Pentecostalism (or stand within the Pentecostal tradition, as in the case of Vineyard congregations), this means offering worshipers an intense religious experience, a feeling that they are in touch with a reality that transcends ordinary, everyday experience. An emphasis on spiritual healing, speaking in tongues, and other gifts of the Spirit is common. In his study of Vineyard, Calvary Chapel, and Hope Chapel churches, Miller (1997) argues that, along with cultural currency, it is their accent on religious experience more than right doctrine that is a primary appeal of these churches. In this emphasis, they seek to overcome the mind-body dualism that is the fruit of the Enlightenment; instead, they honor noncognitive aspects of worship and other moments of intense religious experience that more rationally attuned critics have sometimes derided as "religious enthusiasm." Indeed, whether Pentecostal or not, most posttraditional congregations, and especially those that stand in the African-American tradition, move in this direction, enabling participants to be touched by God's Spirit at a deep level in their being. They encourage a union of head and heart, or, as my Methodist forebear John Wesley put it, a union of "knowledge and vital piety."

When one combines posttraditional congregations' moderate version of strictness (better thought of as seriousness) with the emphases on excellence and religious experience, we come close to the heart of their appeal to many posttraditional individuals, especially Baby Boomers and Generation Xers. By offering clear doctrinal and moral teachings expressed in a contemporary idiom that takes participants' culture seriously, by emphasizing excellence in all aspects of their ministries, and by providing occasions for deep religious experiences, posttraditional congregations offer an appealing religious option among the variety of alternatives available in a detraditionalized "religious marketplace."

Is it possible for mainline congregations to emulate these characteristics in all respects? The answer is almost certainly no. Mainline Protestantism as well as progressive movements within Catholicism have engaged modernity too long and intensely to accept the literalist (or near-literalist) view of the Bible and strict doctrinal teachings of many posttraditional congregations. They also (and I include myself in the "they") value diversity and pluralism too highly.

Furthermore, mainline Protestant congregations and progressive Catholic parishes appeal to a segment of the population that cuts across generational groups and would not likely be attracted to strict churches, not even to the more moderate versions of strictness that we see in many posttraditional congregations. Using survey and case study data, Nancy Ammerman (1997b) has described a significant segment of the church-going population that she calls "Golden Rule Christians," who are much like the "lay liberals" that I mentioned earlier in this chapter. Golden Rule Christians are involved in the church for any or all of the following reasons: because they want the assistance of the church in raising their children, because they believe it important to be related to something or someone that transcends human life, and because they want to be involved in serving others. Such persons, she argues, make up a significant part of the membership of often-thriving mainline Protestant and Catholic congregations that value tolerance and diversity and make minimal demands of belief or behavior on their members. She argues, correctly I believe, that there is not just one but several substantial segments of the American "religious marketplace." There are markets for both high-demand or strict congregations and for low-demand congregations. Some value congregations that limit their choices and state high expectations for them; others value congregations that make more limited demands and permit considerable personal autonomy.[18] Still other restless spiritual seekers remain outside congregations altogether while pursuing their religious quest in a variety of available spiritual boutiques in the religious marketplace.

But does acknowledging this diversity mean that mainline churches are doomed to being the tame, bland, predictable, lukewarm, nondemanding congregations that evangelicals accuse them of being? Does it mean that mainline churches should restrict their appeal to Golden Rule Christians? Does it also mean that Golden Rule Christians can't be moved beyond their "least common denominator" version of Christian life and practice? These are certainly possibilities, especially given the force of inertia in many congregations.

I want to argue, however, that something more is possible. Although most mainline churches will not be able or want to emulate even the somewhat attenuated version of strictness of posttraditional congregations, they can exhibit their own version of seriousness in their ecclesial life, a seriousness that will attract at least some Golden Rule Christians and lead them to a deeper commitment.

What will such seriousness entail? It will differ in some respects from congregation to congregation, reflecting differences of size, resources, and location; yet a number of characteristics can be pointed to, some of which I have already discussed: openness to innovation; strong but shared leadership; attentiveness to the concerns and needs of current and potential participants; and the use of various innovative practices, including small groups, to embody their vision of ministry in culturally appropriate ways. Doing so with an attention to quality and excellence is also part of the equation. Central, however, to all of this is a willingness of serious churches to major in the majors, in particular, unapologetic confession of the authority of the core Christian narrative from scripture—Jesus Christ and him crucified—as truth "for us" that shapes our congregational life and practices. Serious congregations also explore, teach, and demonstrate, with as much clarity and persuasiveness as they can muster, what it means to live one's life reflectively, guided by the Christian story, in posttraditional society.

With these as the majors, mainline congregations can also practice bounded subjectivity when it comes to the minors. We are bound by our commitment to Jesus Christ and him crucified, but open to diversity and faith exploration as to what this means for our individual and corporate lives. An important aid to exploration is emphasis, in ways that are sensitive to contemporary culture, on spiritual practices and disciplines drawn from the Christian tradition (and sometimes borrowed from other traditions). Just as practice is necessary if one is to do anything well, it is crucial if one is to grow in understanding and commitment to the core narrative of the Christian faith or if one is to experience God's presence in the depths of one's being. A non-exhaustive list of such practices includes vital, expressive corporate worship; telling the Christian story through study of the scriptures and the history of the church in ways that relate the story to our experience; disciplines of prayer and meditation; practicing forgiveness; witnessing to others about one's faith; practicing hospitality to each other and to strangers; and working together to serve those in need and to create and maintain just and humane social structures.[19] These practices may not convey the kind of strictness that we find in many of the more evangelical, posttraditional congregations, but such practices are means of growing in faith and expressing a seriousness about the faith one professes. They may even make it possible for lay liberals and Golden Rule Christians to be formed as Christian disciples.

As a more concrete example of what such seriousness might look like in congregational life, consider these excerpts from a letter that I received from the pastor of an "Old First Church" located in a university community in the Midwest. The excitement that he conveys about what is happening in his congregation has come without some of the innovations that posttraditional churches exhibit, but the congregation manifests innovations of its own. Here is some of what he wrote:

> More and more I feel like an anomaly when I read about "the State of the Mainline Churches." I hear talk of changes in worship style which come with post-denominationalism and the declines of old-line churches, but this is far from our experience.
>
> It is almost embarrassing—we keep growing, more young families visit weekly. . . . We want to have "moderate growth" so that we can assimilate our new members and provide appropriate resources. In many ways, we look like the Methodist churches in the Fifties or Sixties: lots of kids in church school, the choir sings classical music, pipe organ is our instrument of choice, there is no screen up front for singing; no drama . . . ; no "seekers' services."
>
> There is considerable talk here about racism and the homeless, and there is action: the building of Habitat houses, the operation of a soup kitchen in our fellowship hall, and the formation of a homeless advocacy group. We find ourselves struggling to be more culturally inclusive. . . . There are alternative worship services planned in the future, but we try to keep a strong base in what we do well. . . .
>
> We are struggling with finances and an old building which needs a million dollars worth of repair. . . . Will we need to diversify our population (currently our largest minority group is Asian-American), provide a strong and enduring culture of spiritual emphasis and spiritual formation, and keep mission efforts focused on building capacity among poor friends rather than on traditional patterns of paternalistic assistance? These are the challenges over the next few years for us.
>
> We give attention to quality . . . ; we simply try to recruit excellent staff, design strong programs, and develop communications which are appropriate—and we see constant improvement. There is an emphasis on small groups—eight Covenant Discipleship Groups have begun in the past year— and youth activities. This would be classified as a liberal church. University students are coming to church in increasing numbers, up 10 or 15 in 1992 to over 100 in

worship now. Why do we not fit the mainline pattern? Or do we? (Amerson 1995)

What is the secret of this congregation's excitement and vitality? We can discern partial answers from some of the things the pastor described. I believe that it comes in large part from the quality of leadership that he and other staff and lay members of the congregation bring to the ministry of that church; the congregation's willingness to be culturally sensitive while continuing to honor many of the church's traditions; their commitment to serving the larger community around them; and their emphasis on providing quality programs, including small groups where people can explore their faith and be formed spiritually. They have not abandoned old practices, but neither do they hold on to them for tradition's sake; they work hard to renew and make their practices vital; and they are willing to innovate. In short, they practice seriousness, not strictness, about the faith and about their congregation's life and ministry.

This mainline congregation is not an anomaly, despite the fact that it is located in the "rust belt" rather than the "sun belt" or even the "Bible belt." What has happened there can happen in other mainline congregations willing to be bold and innovative, who find new wineskins to express an old but ever new message in a twenty-first-century, posttraditional world. The prospect of building such congregations is daunting, but it is also exciting. They are the kind of congregations that have our children and our children's children in view, and they are clearly congregations to which it is worth asking people to make a serious commitment of time, treasure, and talents.

So let me reiterate Karl Barth's words with which I began: "To the distinctiveness of its calling and commission, and therefore to the form of its existence as the people of God in [the] world . . . , there does not correspond in the first instance or intrinsically any absolutely distinctive social form [of the church]." Barth could make this affirmation because he believed that the forms of the church must always be subservient to their function in the service of a God who cannot be captured, cribbed, or confined in any of the institutional structures or traditions that we construct. This is what it means to confess a commitment to *ecclesia semper reformanda*.

Notes

Introduction

1. Cited in Robert W. Lynn and James W. Fraser (1977: 1–2).
2. See especially Dean R. Hoge (1987) on Catholic leadership issues generally and Ruth A. Wallace (1992) on new roles for women in Catholic leadership. See also D'Antonio et al. (1996) for a broad discussion of change in the Catholic Church in America.
3. See Miller (1997) and Sargeant (1996) for discussions of these emerging new groupings that are taking on the functions traditionally carried out by denominations.
4. The "mother" church of the Vineyard Christian Fellowship, led by its founder, John Wimber, recently "disfellowshiped" the Toronto Airport Vineyard Christian Fellowship for excesses in a revival that involved Spirit-induced "holy laughter" and animal laughter to the relative neglect of gifts of charity and compassion. Such a disciplinary action is quite denomination-like in character.

Chapter 1

1. See Michael Ducey's (1977) study of congregations in the Lincoln Park area of Chicago, an area that underwent considerable social upheaval in the 1960s.
2. See Stephen Warner's (1994) helpful discussion of "de facto congregationalism" and its impact on both Christian and non-Christian religious traditions in the United States.
3. Nathan Hatch does not use the term "religious economies," but his interpretation of developments in American Christianity is relatively compatible with this perspective. In their interpretation of American Christianity, which draws in part on Hatch's work, Finke and Stark (1992) describe various religious movements as "winners and losers" based on the ability of groups to remain market sensitive in their practices by offering religious "goods" that appeal to "consumers" who make rational choices among alternatives. Rational choice theory, drawn from classical economics, is adapted to interpret religious markets and the preferences of religious consumers. For various perspectives (pro and con) on the application of rational choice theory to religion, see Lawrence Young (1997). Although I agree with the emphasis on individual choice in matters religious (as well as in other areas of life), I share with other critics a belief that choices are not always as "rational" as the theory holds, and that too much attention is

given to the isolated individual decision maker and not enough to the influence of the relational networks or communities in which decision makers are involved.

4. Many of these changes, whether toward increasing similarity across denominational lines or the development of distinctive niches, are not unique to congregations. They reflect patterns found in various types of contemporary institutions. For discussions of these various cross-institutional patterns, see Powell and DiMaggio (1991).

5. It is beyond my purposes here to pursue the debate over the secularization paradigm. For those wishing to pursue it further, see, for example, David Martin (1978), Bryan Wilson (1985), Stephen Warner (1993), and José Casanova (1994). Wilson is a strong defender of the paradigm; Martin sorts out its various meanings through careful historical analysis and suggests that the concept of secularization is so ambiguous as to warrant being discarded; Warner likewise dismisses the concept as inadequate for understanding religious change in the United States; and Casanova argues that it is useful only if it is considerably revised and limited in its meaning.

6. I find it more useful to use the term "posttraditional" than "postmodern." I do not believe that we have moved beyond modernity, but rather into an advanced or reflexively modern period that has profound implications for the way we relate to tradition. Among those who have written extensively about the transition globally to a posttraditional society is the sociologist Anthony Giddens (e.g., Giddens 1994). This transition is a major characteristic of "late modernity" (which Giddens prefers over "postmodern"). See also two other recent works by Giddens, *The Consequences of Modernity* (1990) and *Modernity and Self-Identity* (1991), in which he discusses similar themes. A similar perspective may be found in Ulrich Beck's idea of a "risk society" characterized by "reflexive modernity" (Beck 1994).

7. For a discussion of the distinction between *traditio* and *traditum*, see Beker (1991). Beker applies *traditio* to the core Pauline tradition of the New Testament, found in the letters that can be attributed directly to Paul. *Traditum* refers to the adaptations of the Pauline core found in the various New Testament documents, such as the Pastoral Epistles, that claimed Pauline authorship but were written later to address new challenges that the early church faced.

8. Cited in Roof and McKinney (1987: 3).

9. Max Weber and others have shown how the great eighth-century Hebrew prophets were key figures in setting in motion the "disenchantment of the world," which includes challenging the sacred traditions and practices of the Hebrew people as well as of surrounding cultures.

10. To be sure, there have been significant changes in family life during the modern period, considerably earlier than the late twentieth century. Many changes occurred during the industrial revolution and especially in the mid to late nineteenth century. Work and home became separate spheres as

male and female roles became increasingly differentiated, at least ideologically, between the workplace (males) and the hearth (females). Much
of what is meant today by the "traditional family" and "family values"
reflects nineteenth-century traditions rather than earlier historical periods.

11. Lyotard argues that after the horrors of the Holocaust and Stalinism, we
can put no credence in the grand narratives of the past with their emphasis
on progress, reason, and science. For Lyotard, the loss of any claim to uni-
versality of these and all metanarratives leads to a kind of social atomism
characteristic of postmodernity. There is no overarching framework, no
grand tradition, in terms of which we can locate ourselves and order our
lives. What we know is relative—locally and individually—and not valid
elsewhere.

12. Several recent writers (e.g. ,Giddens 1990, 1991, 1994; Heelas, Lash, and
Morris 1996) use the term "reflexivity" to refer to what, in reference to
ministry practice, I have called "reflectivity" or "reflective practice" (Carroll 1991).The two terms as I use them, and as used by these other writers,
have a somewhat similar meaning, and I use them interchangeably. I wish
to emphasize that by "reflexivity" I mean not habitual or unthinking behavior, but the exact opposite.

13. John Murray Cuddihy (1978) characterizes American denominational pluralism with the phrase, "I happen to be."

14. Robert Wuthnow's provocative recent book, *After Heaven: Spirituality in
America Since the 1950s* (1998), which was published too late to take into
account in any significant way in this book, makes a similar point applied
to religious belief and practice. He argues that broad social and cultural
changes have led to a lessened importance of what he calls a "spirituality
of dwelling" and a shift to a "spirituality of journey." By the demise of
dwelling, he, like Giddens, emphasizes the impact of disembedding—the
weakening of particular places, communities, extended family, local congregation—on religion.

15. See Timothy Luke (1996) for an extended discussion of the importance of
the destabilizing of social sites for detraditionalization.

16. The data are from a population survey of residents of North Carolina and
southern California, as part of a study of the impact of generational differences on congregations that Wade Clark Roof and I are undertaking.

17. Daniel V. Olson (1993) found in his research that evangelical Protestants
develop strong subcultures that support their religious commitment and
involvement, not because they are primarily "local" in orientation, but
because they choose associates who hold similar conservative religious
beliefs. They share these religiously based ties in a variety of settings outside formal church programs, and such socialization is important in rein-
forcing their beliefs and commitment. Fellowship ties among mainline
Protestants, in contrast, are less dense, more diverse, more privatized, and
thus weaker in their ability to sustain religious beliefs and commitment.

Chapter 2

1. Cimino (1997) also interviewed young adults who had joined traditional
    Catholic parishes and congregations associated with various branches of
    Eastern Orthodoxy. In all cases, he found a selective appropriation of the
    traditions represented. "The young traditionalists clearly embraced choice
    and selectivity in the way they retrieved and identified with their tradi-
    tions" (p. 109).

2. The survey was conducted for Wade Clark Roof and Jackson W. Carroll in
    February 1997 by FGI Integrated Marketing, Chapel Hill, North Carolina,
    as part of a study of the impact of generational differences on congrega-
    tions. The research is funded by a grant from the Lilly Endowment, Inc.

3. William V. D'Antonio (Jones 1995: 3) is currently undertaking a study of
    small Christian communities among U.S. Catholics. Although many such
    groups are parish-based and -sponsored, many as a result of the Renew pro-
    gram (see Kelly 1991), some, like those studied by Voyé, are autonomous,
    independent of the Catholic Church.

4. See Garrett Paul (1993) for a helpful summary of Troeltsch's position. See
    also Ralph Hood's discussion of Troeltsch and mysticism (Hood 1985).

5. Miller gives detailed descriptions of these three movements and reflects on
    their implications for mainline Protestantism.

6. Some of these visits have been for the purpose of field research for the pro-
    ject (see above, n. 2) on the impact of generational differences on congre-
    gations. I draw on my own field notes from these visits as well as on those
    by students who have worked with us in the project.

7. See Lyle E. Schaller's (1993) edited collection of case studies of thriving
    center-city congregations, most of which can be characterized as posttra-
    ditional in their style. Most examples in the collection are from conserva-
    tive churches. Only a few are liberal in their theology and ministry. Several
    others combine a more conservative theological stance with a liberal social
    justice mission agenda.

8. I am drawing once more on Wacker's (1995) characterization of Pente-
    costals as both primitivists and pragmatists and applying these categories
    to leaders of these new-style churches.

9. In politics we also have had two recent presidents, both Southern Baptists,
    who preferred the familiar form of their first names: Jimmy Carter and Bill
    Clinton. Both have been populist in style.

10. See Laurence Moore's *Selling God* (1994) for a fascinating historical
    account of consumerism in American religion.

11. Willow Creek has developed a special ministry to members of Generation
    X; and New Song founder, Dieter Zander, has joined the Willow Creek
    staff, with developing this new ministry as a primary responsibility.

12. Scott Thumma (1996: 434–39) distinguishes three types of megachurch
    architecture: *nontraditional*, which is mostly what I am describing here;
    conventional (using traditional architectural forms but expressed on a
    megascale); and *composite,* a mixture of contemporary and traditional

forms.

13. Field notes by Shawn Landres from New Song Church, 1996. In a subsequent visit, however, one of the staff told us that they are now trying to buy property to build a church building. The weekly process of setting up and then breaking down seats, stage, and media equipment in the school gymnasium has become too difficult and time consuming.

14. A joke making the rounds in evangelical circles is that a praise chorus is four words, three lines, and two hours.

15. This discussion of commitment draws on the work of Scott Thumma (1996: 452ff.).

16. C. Eric Lincoln and Lawrence Mamiya (1990: 2–7) refer to this heritage as the "black sacred cosmos."

17. See the history of Bethel by Mamiya (1994).

Chapter 3

1. In his autobiography, the Methodist circuit rider Peter Cartwright (1856) lampooned an educated ministry, referring to seminary-educated preachers as being like "lettuce growing under the shade of a peach tree, or like a gosling that had got the straddles by wading in the dew." Some years later, as the Methodist Episcopal Church, South, was debating the founding of a seminary at Vanderbilt, a minority report tried to veto the plan. The tradition of theological schools, the report stated, "has little that is favorable to Methodism, and much that is adverse. [Seminaries] have been fruitful sources of heresies innumerable, of a manner of preaching not generally desirable and rarely effectual among us, and of that formalism that never favors experiential religion" (cited in Michaelson 1956: 276).

2. A congregational study earlier than Warner's by Michael Ducey (1977) contrasts the worship styles of several urban congregations in Chicago. Ducey's book, *Sunday Morning: Aspects of Urban Ritual*, contrasts what he calls "mass ritual," which is traditional or institutional in character, with "interaction ritual," which is more egalitarian and Spirit-led. Interestingly, those congregations practicing interaction ritual were not evangelicals nor did they have large memberships. They were liberal Protestant congregations who believed that new urban realities call for new and innovative, nonhierarchical worship patterns and other ecclesial practices.

3. For a discussion of Paul's use of tradition and also of other New Testament writers who claimed the authority of Paul for their writings, see Beker (1991).

4. Obviously the narratives of tradition/order and freedom are not the only two in the Christian heritage. I have chosen to emphasize them because of their pertinence to these chapters.

5. The New Testament scholar Gerd Lüdemann (1995: 148ff.) argues a different thesis regarding Marcion. While acknowledging Marcion's excesses, Lüdemann believes that Marcion's emphasis on the newness of the gospel, on the gospel as a gift of grace, and on faith as freedom from the Mosaic

law was in the spirit of Jesus; thus Marcion deserves a fresh hearing.

6. See the very helpful discussion of characteristics of tradition—"deep symbols" as he calls them—by Edward Farley (1996: 3–8).
7. Cited in Schreiter (1985: 110).

Chapter 4

1. In the first congregation I served as a pastor, I used several ancient hymns of the church that were unfamiliar to the congregation. Although I explained the background of the hymns and had the choir rehearse them with the congregation, I received several angry notes from members. One said, "Please quit singing these *new* hymns. Let's go back to the old, traditional hymns like 'Blessed Assurance' and 'In the Garden.'" The note is a reminder that tradition is often what one is accustomed to rather than something that is old.
2. I am indebted for this example to one of my students at Duke Divinity School, Marty Cauley, who did an analysis of Hillsborough United Methodist Church as part of a class assignment.
3. It would be a mistake, however, to think that the founding leaders of a new congregation are totally free to do as they please, even when they are independent churches. They and their potential constituents carry in their heads images of what a congregation should be and do, and it is difficult to stray too far from these accepted ideas.
4. Peter Drucker (1989: 5) maintains that the training and widespread use of volunteer leadership is one of the major lessons that business leaders can learn from nonprofits, especially from leaders of "pastoral" or posttraditional churches. "The steady transformation of the volunteer from well-meaning amateur to trained, professional, unpaid staff member is the most significant development in the nonprofit sector—as well as the one with the most far-reaching implications for tomorrow's businesses."
5. See Hybels and Hybels 1995: 149–50.
6. Cited in Mouw 1994: 8.
7. Wimber 1983: 19 (cited in Shibley 1996: 85).
8. A testimony to the importance of "consulting the faithful" comes from an example outside the church. An article in *The Atlantic Monthly* (Kuntsler 1996) on town and city planning, reflecting what is called the new urbanist movement, describes a strategy called a "charette" now being used by new urban planners. It is a professional design workshop held for the purpose of land development or redevelopment that includes public meetings that bring all parties, including local citizens, together in one room to get the issues on the table and to produce drawings and plans.
9. The experience of the hymnal revision committee of the United Methodist Church is instructive. The new hymnal has been extremely positively received, with almost 95 percent of the congregations now using it. This is in sharp contrast to a 1964 revision that was not nearly so widely accepted and that was undertaken with much less consultation with the whole

church. The new hymnal's acceptance in large part is the result of the process of listening to rank-and-file clergy and laity through surveys and hearings. A defining moment came in the much-debated decision to restore several favorite hymns, especially "Onward Christian Soldiers." Carlton R. Young, the hymnal's general editor, describes what happened:

> In reversing itself the committee was perceived as responsive to the will of the majority, a view in sharp contrast to the way that the multitudes regarded some church agencies and the church's general political structure. From that time forward the committee was for the multifarious majority a trusted and responsive ally in the war against United Methodism's repressive and impervious bureaucratic superstructure. The committee's work was applauded as an open and an honest attempt to do the will of the church. . . . The resolution of this controversy in favor of "the people" contributed to the ongoing approval of the work of the Hymnal Revision Committee, its acceptance at General Conference, and in turn the sale and acceptance of the hymnal (Young 1993: 137).

The committee did not avoid developing theological and musicological criteria or making hard judgments about many texts and tunes. But they also listened and took seriously the wisdom from the congregations. The result was a pluralistic hymnal that has been widely accepted by a pluralistic denomination.

10. Several authors have addressed these issues in some depth. See Schreiter (1985: 122–43), Sample (1990), and Mouw (1994).

11. See Penny Becker's unpublished paper, "Mining the Tradition: Social Change and Culture Work in Two Protestant Congregations" (1994), for an example of a Baptist congregation in suburban Chicago that was able to incorporate multicultural worship traditions by recognizing the importance of sharing in each other's traditions.

12. When I was giving lectures at a faculty of theology in Sweden, I was told by one of the faculty members that many of their students were so attracted to the Taizé meditative style of worship, which typically excludes a sermon, that they had no interest in learning how to preach. They much preferred worship that was limited to prayer and singing. For background on the Taizé community and its practices, see Taizé (1998).

13. See Thomas and Jardine (1994) for a case study of the use of small groups in a large evangelical congregation.

14. Wigger (1994: 51–52) cites John Leith's interpretation of Calvin's position on this point.

15. See Olson (1994) for a case study of a Disciple Bible Study group in a United Methodist congregation.

16. See, for example, the work of Finke and Stark (1992) and Iannacone (1994). One of the ways they have extended the Kelley thesis is by incorporating it

into rational choice theory drawn from classical economics. For perspectives on the pros and cons of applying rational choice theory to religion, see Lawrence Young (1997).

17. See Christian Smith's (1998: 89ff.) interpretation of evangelicalism using what he calls a "subcultural identity" theory of evangelical strength in contrast to strictness theory. See also Perrin and Mauss (1993) for a discussion of the limits of strictness theory as applied to congregations of the Vineyard Christian Fellowship.

18. Perhaps the extreme example of openness that I have experienced was in a mainline congregation in an affluent suburb of a major city. When an adult presented himself for baptism, he was asked by the pastor: "Do you confess belief in Jesus Christ, whatever that may mean to you?"

19. See, for example, Dykstra (1989), Bass (1997), and Wuthnow (1998) for fuller discussion of the range and meaning of various Christian practices.

Works Cited

Amerson, Philip. 1995. Personal correspondence, 17 March.

Ammerman, Nancy Tatom. 1987. *Bible Believers: Fundamentalists in the Modern World*. New Brunswick, N.J.: Rutgers University Press.

———. 1997a. *Congregation and Community*. New Brunswick, N.J.: Rutgers University Press.

———. "Golden Rule Christianity." 1997b. In *Lived Religion in America*, edited by David Hall, 196–216. Princeton: Princeton University Press.

Ault, James, and Michael Camerini. 1987. *Born Again: Life in a Fundamentalist Baptist Church*. James Ault Films.

Barth, Karl. 1956. *Church Dogmatics, IV/1:The Doctrine of Reconciliation*, translated by G. W. Bromiley. Edinburgh: T. & T. Clark.

———. 1962. *Church Dogmatics, IV/3/2: The Doctrine of Reconciliation*, translated by G. W. Bromiley. Edinburgh: T. & T. Clark.

Bass, Dorothy C., ed. 1997. *Practicing Our Faith*. San Francisco: Jossey-Bass.

Bauman, Zygmunt. 1995. *Life in Fragments: Essays in Postmodern Morality*. Oxford: Blackwell.

Beck, Ulrich. 1994. "The Reinvention of Politics: Toward a Theory of Reflexive Modernization." In *Reflexive Modernization: Politics, Tradition and Aesthetics in the Modern Social Order*, by Ulrich Beck, Anthony Giddens, and Scott Lash. Stanford, Cal.: Stanford University Press.

Becker, Penny Edgell. 1994. "Mining the Tradition: Social Change and Culture Work in Two Protestant Congregations." Unpublished paper.

Beker, J. Christiaan. 1991. *Heirs of Paul: Paul's Legacy in the New Testament and in the Church Today*. Minneapolis: Fortress Press.

Bellah, Robert, et al. 1985. *Habits of the Heart: Individualism and Commitment in American Life*. Berkeley: University of California Press.

Bellamy, Edward. 1888. *Looking Backward, 2000–1887*. Boston: Ticknor.

Berger, Peter L. 1992. *A Far Glory: The Quest for Faith in an Age of Credulity*. New York: Free Press.

———. 1998. "Protestantism and the Quest for Certainty." *The Christian Century* 115, no. 23: 782–85.

Brown, Raymond E. 1984. *The Churches the Apostles Left Behind*. New York: Paulist.

Burnett, John. 1997. "All Things Considered." *National Public Radio*, 28 January.

Carroll, Jackson W. 1991. *As One with Authority: Reflective Leadership in Ministry*. Louisville: Westminster/John Knox.

Carroll, Jackson W., Douglas W. Johnson, and Martin E. Marty. 1979. *Religion in America—1950 to the Present*. San Francisco: Harper and Row.

Cartwright, Peter. 1856. *Autobiography of Peter Cartwright, the Backwoods Preacher*, edited by W. P. Strickland. New York: The Methodist Book Concern.

Casanova, José. 1994. *Public Religions in the Modern World*. Chicago: University of Chicago Press.

Chesterton, G. K. 1909. *Orthodoxy*. New York: J. Lane.

Cimino, Richard P. 1997. *Against the Stream: The Adoption of Traditional Christian Faiths by Young People*. Lanham, Md.: University Press of America.

Coalter, Milton J., John M. Mulder, and Louis B. Weeks. 1996. *Vital Signs: The Promise of Mainstream Protestantism*. Grand Rapids: Eerdmans.

Cuddihy, John Murray. 1978. *No Offense: Civil Religion and Protestant Taste*. New York: Seabury.

D'Antonio, William V., James D. Davidson, Dean R. Hoge, and Ruth A. Wallace. 1996. *Laity American and Catholic: Transforming the Church*. Kansas City: Sheed and Ward.

Davidman, Lynn. 1991. *Tradition in a Rootless World*. Berkeley: University of California Press.

Davie, Jodiy Shapiro. 1995. *Women in the Presence: Constructing Community and Seeking Spirituality in Mainline Protestantism*. Philadelphia: University of Pennsylvania Press.

Dawn, Marva J. 1995. *Reaching Out without Dumbing Down: A Theology of Worship for the Turn-of-the-Century Culture*. Grand Rapids: Eeerdmans.

Dobbelaere, Karel. 1991. Personal conversation.

Drucker, Peter F. 1989. "What Business Can Learn from Nonprofits." *Harvard Business Review* 89, no. 4 (July-August): 88–93.

———. 1990. "The New Models." *Next* 1, no. 2 (August): 1–2.

Ducey, Michael H. 1977. *Sunday Morning: Aspects of Urban Ritual*. Chicago: University of Chicago Press.

Durkheim, Emile. 1912. *The Elementary Forms of the Religious Life*, translated by Joseph Swain. Reprint, New York: Free Press, 1954.

Dykstra, Craig. 1989. *Growing in the Life of Christian Faith*. Louisville: Theology and Worship Ministry Unit, Presbyterian Church (U.S.A.).

Dykstra, Craig, and James Hudnut-Beumler. 1992. *The Organizational Revolution: Presbyterians and American Denominationalism*, edited by Milton J. Coalter, John M. Mulder, and Louis B. Weeks. Louisville: Westminster/John Knox.

Eiesland, Nancy L., and R. Stephen Warner. 1998. "Ecology: Seeing the Congregation in Context." In *Studying Congregations: A New Handbook*, edited by Nancy T. Ammerman et al., 40–77. Nashville: Abingdon.

Farley, Edward. 1996. *Deep Symbols: Their Postmodern Effacement and Reclamation*. Valley Forge, Pa.: Trinity Press International.

Finke, Roger, and Rodney Stark. 1992. *The Churching of America, 1776–1990: Winners and Losers in Our Religious Economy*. New Brunswick, N.J.: Rutgers University Press.

Fitzgerald, Frances. 1986. *Cities on a Hill*. New York: Simon and Schuster.

Freedman, Samuel G. 1993. *Upon This Rock: The Miracles of a Black Church*. New York: HarperCollins.

Giddens, Anthony. 1990. *The Consequences of Modernity.* Cambridge, England: Polity.

———. 1991. *Modernity and Self-Identity.* Cambridge, England: Polity.

———. 1994. "Living in a Post-Traditional Society." In *Reflexive Modernization,* by Ulrich Beck, Anthony Giddens, and Scott Lash, 56–109. Stanford: Stanford University Press.

Green, Arthur. 1994. *Judaism for the Post-Modern Era.* Samuel H. Goldenson Lecture. Cincinnati: Hebrew Union College-Jewish Institute of Religion.

Hatch, Nathan O. 1989. *The Democratization of American Christianity.* New Haven: Yale University Press.

Hauerwas, Stanley, and William H. Willimon. 1989. *Resident Aliens.* Nashville: Abingdon.

———. 1996. *Where Resident Aliens Live: Exercises for Christian Practice.* Nashville: Abingdon.

Heelas, Paul, Scott Lash, and Paul Morris, eds. 1996. *Detraditionalization: Critical Reflections on Authority and Identity.* Oxford: Blackwell.

Heifetz, Ronald A. 1994. *Leadership Without Easy Answers.* Cambridge: Harvard University Press.

Hervieu-Léger, Daniele. 1994. "Modernity, Secularization, and Religious Memory in Western Europe." Paper presented at the annual meeting of the Association for the Sociology of Religion.

Hoge, Dean R., Benton Johnson, and Donald A. Luidens. 1994. *Vanishing Boundaries: The Religion of Mainline Protestant Baby Boomers.* Louisville: Westminster/John Knox.

Holifield, E. Brooks. 1994. "Toward a History of American Congregations." In *American Congregations, Vol. 2, New Perspectives in the Study of Congregations,* edited by James P. Wind and James W. Lewis, 23–53. Chicago: University of Chicago Press.

Hood, Ralph W., Jr. 1995. "Mysticism." In *The Sacred in a Secular Age.* Edited by Phillip E. Hammond, 285–97. Berkeley: University of California Press.

Hybels, Lynne, and Bill Hybels. 1995. *Rediscovering Church: The Story and Vision of Willow Creek Community Church.* Grand Rapids: Zondervan.

Iannacone, Lawrence. 1994. "Why Strict Churches Are Strong." *American Journal of Sociology* 99: 1180–1211.

Jones, Arthur. 1995. "Small Christian Communities Alive and Varied." *National Catholic Reporter* 31, no.36: 3.

Kelley, Dean M. 1972. *Why Conservative Churches Are Growing.* San Francisco: Harper and Row.

Kelly, James R. 1991. "Community and Contentiousness: Lessons from the Renew Program." In *Carriers of Faith,* edited by Carl S. Dudley, Jackson W. Carroll, and James P. Wind, 171–82. Louisville: Westminster/John Knox.

Kuntsler, James Howard. 1996. "Home from Nowhere." *The Atlantic Monthly* 278, no. 3: 43–66.

Lincoln, C. Eric, and Lawrence H. Mamiya. 1990. *The Black Church in the African American Experience.* Durham, N.C.: Duke University Press.

Lindbeck, George. 1984. *The Nature of Doctrine: Religion and Theology in a Postliberal Age*. Philadelphia: Westminster.

Luckmann, Thomas. 1967. *The Invisible Religion*. New York: Macmillan.

Lüdemann, Gerd. 1996. *Heretics: The Other Side of Early Christianity*, translated by John Bowden. Louisville: Westminster/John Knox.

Luke, Timothy. 1996. "Identity, Meaning and Globalization: Detraditionalization in Postmodern Space-Time Compression." In *Detraditionalization: Critical Reflections on Authority and Identity*, edited by Paul Heelas, Scott Lash, and Paul Morris, 109–33. Oxford: Blackwell.

Lynn, Robert W. and James W. Fraser. 1977. "Images of the Small Church in American History." In *Small Churches Are Beautiful.* Edited by Jackson W. Carroll, 1-19. San Francisco: Harper and Row.

Lyotard, Jean-François. 1984. *The Post-Modern Condition*. Minneapolis: University of Minnesota Press.

MacIntyre, Alasdair. 1984. *After Virtue*. 2d ed.Notre Dame, Ind.: University of Notre Dame Press.

Mamiya, Lawrence H. 1994. "A Social History of the Bethel African Methodist Episcopal Church in Baltimore: The House of God and the Struggle for Freedom." In *American Congregations*. Vol. 1, *Portraits of Twelve Religious Communities*, edited by James P. Wind and James W. Lewis, 221–92. Chicago: University of Chicago Press.

Mandela, Nelson. 1994. *Long Walk to Freedom*. New York: Little, Brown.

Martin, David A. 1978. *A General Theory of Secularlization*. New York: Harper and Row.

Maudlin, Michael, and Edward Gilbreath. 1994. "'Selling Out the House of God?'" *Christianity Today* 38, no. 8: 21–25.

Meagher, John C. 1990. *The Truing of Christianity, Visions of Life and Thought for the Future*. New York: Doubleday.

Mellado, James. 1996. *Willow Creek Community Church*. Case #9–691–102. Boston: Harvard Business School Publishing, 23 January.

Michaelson, Robert S. 1956. "The Protestant Ministry in America: 1980 to the Present." In *The Ministry in Historical Perspective*, edited by H. Richard Niebuhr and Daniel Day Williams, 250–87. New York: Harper and Row.

Miller, Donald E. 1993. "Postmodern Characteristics of Three Rapidly Growing Christian Movements: Calvary Chapel, Vineyard Christian Fellowship, and Hope Chapel." Paper presented at the annual meeting of the Society for the Scientific Study of Religion. Raleigh, N.C., 29–31 October.

———. 1997. *Reinventing American Protestantism: Christianity in the New Millennium*. Berkeley: University of California Press.

Moore, R. Laurence. 1994. *Selling God: American Religion in the Marketplace of Culture*. New York: Oxford University Press.

Mouw, Richard J. 1994. *Consulting the Faithful*. Grand Rapids: Eerdmans.

Noll, Mark A. 1994. *The Scandal of the Evangelical Mind*. Grand Rapids: Eerdmans.

O'Keefe, Mark. 1996. "Marketing Methodism." *The Oregonian*, 23 October, pp. C1, C9.

Olson, Daniel V. 1993. "Fellowship Ties and the Transmission of Religious Identity." In *Beyond Establishment: Protestant Identity in a Post-Protestant Age*, edited by Jackson W. Carroll and Wade Clark Roof, 32–53. Louisville: Westminster/John Knox.

————. 1994. "Making Disciples in a Liberal Protestant Church." In *"I Come Away Stronger": How Small Groups Are Shaping American Religion*, edited by Robert Wuthnow, 125–47. Grand Rapids: Eerdmans.

Paul, Garrett E. 1993. "Why Troeltsch? Why Today? Theology for the 21st Century." *The Christian Century* 110, no. 20: 676–79.

Perrin, Robin D, and Armand L. Mauss. 1993. "Strictly Speaking . . . ; Kelley's Quandary and the Vineyard Christian Fellowship." *Journal for the Scientific Study of Religion* 32: 125–34.

Powell, Walter W., and Paul J. DiMaggio, eds. *The New Institutionalism in Organizational Analysis*. Chicago: University of Chicago Press, 1991.

Roof, Wade Clark. 1993. *A Generation of Seekers: The Spiritual Journeys of the Baby Boom Generation*. San Francisco: HarperSanFrancisco.

Roof, Wade Clark, and William McKinney. 1987. *American Mainline Religion*. New Brunswick, N.J.: Rutgers University Press.

Sample, Tex. 1990. *U.S. Lifestyles and Mainline Churches*. Louisville: Westminster/John Knox.

Sargeant, Kimon H. 1996. "The Post-Modern Denomination: An Organizational Analysis of the Willow Creek Association." Paper presented at the annual meeting of the Religious Research Association. Nashville, November.

Schaller, Lyle E. 1992. *The Seven-Day-a-Week Church*. Nashville: Abingdon.

————. 1996. *Tattered Trust*. Nashville: Abingdon.

Schaller, Lyle E., ed. 1993. *Center City Churches: The New Urban Frontier*. Nashville: Abingdon.

Schattauer, Thomas H. 1994. "A Clamor for the Contemporary: The Present Challenge for Baptismal Identity and Liturgical Tradition in American Culture." Paper presented at the region 1 conference of the Association of Lutheran Church Musicians. Yale University, 27 July.

Schreiter, Robert J. 1985. *Constructing Local Theologies*. Maryknoll, N.Y.: Orbis.

Schweizer, Eduard. 1961. *Church Order in the New Testament*, translated by Frank Clarke. Studies in Biblical Theology 1/32. London: SCM.

Shibley, Mark A. 1996. *Resurgent Evangelicalism in the United States*. Columbia: University of South Carolina Press.

Smith, Christian. 1998.*American Evangelicalism: Embattled and Thriving*. Chicago: University of Chicago Press.

Stark, William M, in consultation with Raymond H. Swartzback. 1993. "A Multi-Cultural Church in a Multi-Cultural Community. " In *Center City Churches: The New Urban Frontier*. Edited by Lyle E. Schaller, 99-108. Nashville: Abingdon.

Swidler, Ann. 1986 "Culture in Action: Symbols and Strategies." *American Sociological Review* 51: 273–86.

"Taize Community." 1998. <http://www.taize.fr>.

Thomas, George M., and Douglas S. Jardine. 1994. "Jesus and Self in Everyday Life: Individual Spirituality through a Small Group in a Large Church." In *"I Come Away Stronger": How Small Groups Are Shaping American Religion*, edited by Robert Wuthnow, 275–99. Grand Rapids: Eerdmans.

Thumma, Scott L. 1996. "The Kingdom, the Power, and the Glory: The Megachurch in Modern American Society." Ph.D. diss., Emory University.

Tillich, Paul. 1948. *The Protestant Era*, translated by James Luther Adams. Chicago: University of Chicago Press.

Troeltsch, Ernst. 1912. *The Social Teachings of the Christian Church*, translated by Olive Wyon. Reprint, Louisville: Westminster/John Knox, 1992.

Trueheart, Charles. 1996. "The Next Church." *The Atlantic Monthly* 278, no. 2 (August): 37–58.

Voyé, Liliane. 1995. "From Institutional Catholicism to 'Communities of Inspiration': Another Look at Belgium." In *The Post-War Generation and Establishment Religion: Cross-Cultural Perspectives*, edited by Wade Clark Roof, Jackson W. Carroll, and David A. Roozen, 191–206. Boulder, Colo.: Westview.

Wacker, Grant. 1995. "Searching for Eden with a Satellite Dish: Primitivism, Pragmatism, and the Pentecostal Character." In *The Primitive Church in the Modern World*, edited by Richard T. Hughes, 139–66. Urbana: University of Illinois Press.

Wallace, Ruth A. 1992. *They Call Her Pastor: A New Role for Catholic Women*. Albany, N.Y.: State University of New York Press.

Warner, R. Stephen. 1988. *New Wine in Old Wineskins: Evangelicals and Liberals in a Small-Town Church*. Berkeley: University of California Press.

———. 1994. "The Place of the Congregation in the Contemporary American Religious Configuration." In *American Congregations*. Vol. 2, *New Perspectives in the Study of Congregations*, edited by James P. Wind and James W. Lewis, 54–99. Chicago: University of Chicago Press.

———. 1993. "Work in Progress Toward a New Paradigm for the Sociological Study of Religion in the United States." *American Journal of Sociology* 5: 1044–93.

Weber, Max. 1968. *Economy and Society: An Outline of Interpretive Sociology*, translated by Ephraim Fischoff et al., edited by Guenther Roth and Claus Wittich. 2 vols. New York: Bedminister Press.

Wells, David F. 1993. *No Place for Truth, or, Whatever Happened to Evangelical Theology?* Grand Rapids: Eerdmans.

Wigger, J. Bradley. 1994. "Gracious Words: A Presbyterian Bible Study." In *"I Come Away Stronger": How Small Groups Are Shaping American Religion*, edited by Robert Wuthnow, 37–54. Grand Rapids: Eerdmans.

Williams, Colin W. 1968. "The Church." *New Directions in Theology Today* 4. Philadelphia: Westminster.

Wilson, Bryan. 1995. "Secularization: the Inherited Model." In *The Sacred in a Secular Age*. Edited by Phillip E. Hammond, 1–20. Berkeley: University of California Press.

Wimber, John. 1983. "Zip to 3,000 in 5 Years: Part II." In *Signs and Wonders Today*, compiled by the editors of *Christian Life Magazine*, 18–21. Wheaton, Ill.: Christian Life Magazine.

Winter, Miriam Therese, Adair Lummis, and Allison Stokes. 1994. *Defecting in Place*. New York: Crossroad.

Wuthnow, Robert. 1994. *Sharing the Journey: Support Groups and America's New Quest for Community*. New York: Free Press.

———. 1998. *After Heaven: Spirituality in America Since the 1950s*. Berkeley: University of California Press.

York, Michael. 1992. *The Glory and the Power: Remaking the World.* PBS Video, WETA, Washington, D.C.

Young, Carlton R. 1993. *Companion to the United Methodist Hymnal.* Nashville: Abingdon.

Young, Lawrence A., ed. 1997. *Rational Choice Theory and Religion.* New York: Routledge.

Index

Abraham, 60
Abrahamson, Jim, 44, 46, 82–83, 84
accommodation to detraditionaliza-
  tion, 34–37
Acts of the Apostles, 39, 53, 58, 97
African Americans, 44, 49–50, 73,
  84–85, 97, 107 n.16
African Methodist Episcopal
  (A.M.E.) church, xi, 49–50
After Heaven (Wuthnow), 105 n.14
After Virtue (MacIntyre), 14, 74
AIDS Ministry, 48
Alabama, 84
A.M.E. church. *See* African Metho-
  dist Episcopal (A.M.E.) church
American Revolution, 61
Amerson, Philip, 100
Ammerman, Nancy, 30, 86–87, 98
angels, 73
Anglican Church, 61, 71
Antioch church, 58
Antiochian Orthodox Church, xi,
  33, 91
architecture, 43–44, 52, 64, 78, 106
  n.12
Arizona, 45
Asbury, Francis, 14
Assemblies of God, xi, 33
Atlanta, Ga., 23–24
Augsburg Confession, 70
Augustine, 65, 72
Ault, James, 32
authority
  of Bible, 32, 96
  and detraditionalization, 16–17,
    21, 26
  of leaders of posttraditional con-
    gregations, 85–86

of traditions, 69, 71, 82
  See also traditions

Baby Boomers, 6, 24, 25, 42–43,
  49, 53, 56, 74, 79, 90, 91, 94, 97
Baby Busters, 24, 53, 90. *See also*
  Generation Xers
Bach, Johann S., 45
Baltimore, Md., 49
baptism, 13, 46, 55, 58, 67, 110
  n.18
Baptist Church
  African Americans in, 49
  after American Revolution, 61
  in Georgia, 23
  Great Awakening and, 3
  in Illinois, 109 n.11
  in New York, 84–85
  posttraditional congregation of,
    84–85
  second-generation Baptists, 62
  U.S. presidents as Southern Bap-
    tist, 106 n.9
  in Virginia, 31
Barnabas, 58
Barth, Karl, 1–2, 5, 25, 53, 67, 88,
  101
Basic Christian Communities, xi
Bass, Dorothy, 110 n.19
Bauman, Zygmunt, 19, 24
Becker, Penny, 109 n.11
Beck, Ulrich, 104 n.6
Beker, J. Christiaan, 104 n.7, 107
  n.3
Belgium, 35, 36
Bellah, Robert, 34
Bellamy, Edward, ix, xiii, 76
Berger, Peter, 9, 22

Willimon, William, 27
Willow Creek Community Church
    (Ill.), x, xii, 6, 27, 38, 40, 42–44,
    46, 47, 48, 52, 55–56, 96, 106 n.11
Wilson, Bryan, 104 n.5
Wimber, John, 40, 89, 103 n.4, 108
    n.7
Windsor Village United Methodist
    Church, 49
Womanchurch movement, xi
worship practices
    alternative worship generally, x
    liturgical renewal movement, 5,
        56
    multicultural worship, 100, 109
        n.11

"niche" congregations and, 7
in posttraditional congregations,
    44–46, 52, 56–57, 77–78
seeker services, 43, 46, 52, 56
U.S. history of, 2–5
weeknight services, 46
See also music
Wuthnow, Robert, x-xi, 36, 78, 105
    n.14, 110 n.19

Young, Carlton R., 109 n.9
Young, Lawrence, 103 n.3, 110 n.16
Youngblood, Johnny Ray, 84–85

Zander, Dieter, 40, 106 n.11